Aliens

The Strange Truth

Dictation from The Great White Brotherhood

Bob Sanders

DISCLAIMERS

COPYRIGHT

TABLE OF CONTENTS

FOREWORD

So far in this series of books we have attempted to present information concerning the origins of all life in a fairly logical order, so that anyone interested in the subject would be able to comprehend.

However, as we have mentioned on a number of occasions, life is complex and there are aspects of it that do not necessarily follow in a chronological order.

Indeed, there are aspects of life so far remote from anything that even the most advanced, even the most open-minded person would not be able to accept.

However, we have been tasked by those above us, to attempt to explain as much as we can about life so that, as we all move into Ascension, we can all have a firm foundation of facts upon which to build the Ascension process.

To rise in spirituality, implies rising in wisdom and wisdom is based on knowledge, so we hope that you can appreciate that we need to explain as much as we hope you are able of comprehending.

We have already talked at length about a number of aspects of life that have been ignored or unknown until the publication of the books so far made available to you and we intend to continue to release information until all who wish to advance may do so.

You cannot advance while you are being kept in the dark, so to speak, so we will shine more and more light into the mysteries of creation, so that you may stand shoulder to shoulder with the giants.

Which brings us to the subject of this book, which will be number five in the series.

The subject of this book will be the origins of life, not as we have described it in any of the previous books but from an aspect, we feel, has never been discussed before.

As we mentioned, life is complex and we have already attempted to describe how life is created in an enormous kindergarten, in book 4.

Then we have described how all the dimensions were created and life placed in them. We followed this train of thought by describing as clearly as we could the various aspects of intelligent life, Higher Self, Imagination, Logos and many other aspects including the strange concept that we all live in an imaginary world.

One would think that we have covered the gamut of life, but it is not so.

There are other aspects that we may consider and, in this book, we will try to explain an aspect of life that is relatively unknown.

So, as always, we ask you to be as open-minded as you can and allow this information to flow into you, even if you cannot immediately understand the concepts.

You will understand one day and will grow in wisdom.

CHAPTER 1

DIMENSIONS DISSECTED

As we mentioned in the Foreword, we intend to devote this book to a study of an aspect of life that has seldom ever been mentioned in the past and we are concerned that even today there will be many people unable to comprehend the message.
But that is not our concern. We are tasked with revealing information and so we will make this information available now and hope that some, at least, will comprehend. Others will begin to understand at a later date.

So, what are we going to talk about, what aspect of life is of such concern?
Quite simply, we wish to discuss with you, to review, an aspect of life that is considered to be imaginary by many.

We wish to explain to you that those beings that you call extra-terrestrials are, in fact, an aspect of you that life creates in inter-dimensions that are, nevertheless connected to you and, in fact, are you.

So, we will appear to be talking, largely, about extra-terrestrial beings, entities that, nevertheless, are connected to you, and are you.

So, we will be describing extra-terrestrial beings, entities that, nevertheless, are you but in a different form - both the good and the bad ones. They are a reflection of the good and the bad that are incarnate at the moment, have been in the past or will be in the future.

You are all, we are sure, familiar with the concept of alien life forms of various types that have been visiting your planet for a long period of time. These aliens tell your authorities that they have come from various planets in the solar system as we have mentioned in other works. They once said that they came from the moon but, once man found out they did not, they said they came from Mars. When man found out that this was not true they began to claim that they came from star clusters further and further away knowing full well that these places could not be verified by anyone.

All of this is just a tissue of lies.
They come from areas that we would refer to as interdimensional. That is to say, the areas between dimensions.

Now, this is going to be very difficult to describe in simple terms and so we intend to devote this complete book to these so-called aliens and where they originated, because this knowledge will shed light on humanity as you know it - as you are living it now - and will broaden your knowledge of your existence because, as we said, they are actually creations of your imagination and, although they appear as real as your world does to you now, in fact they are all a very bizarre and intricate aspect of life.

The problem, as always, is where to begin?

Perhaps you will forgive us if we give a resumé of life, as we have previously mentioned it in other works, or at least part of what we have told you, especially concentrating on dimensions and how they affect life as you live it now.

So, we have mentioned that God's Archangels created eight dimensions. We have explained that within each dimension there are many sub-dimensions, each one contained within a coating of thin gravity to keep each sub-dimension separate from any other and that each dimension was it self contained within a coating of thick gravity to ensure that each dimension was kept apart from any other of the eight dimensions.

And we have described in some detail the various dimensions that harbour life.

Now, we do not wish to waste too much time in repeating that which we have explained in other works, and so, for those who have not studied these other books, we suggest you do because, as we have also previously stated, these books, although they might appear from their titles to be unconnected, in fact have been carefully chosen and presented in order. So, they should be regarded as one giant compendium, each one following on from where the previous one left off.

So, we assume that you have read, studied and digested what we said about dimensions, because we are now going to take an in-depth look at a dimension and try to expose to the light of day what exactly they are and try to expose also some of the lifeforms that live amongst the maze of sub-dimensions because, don't think for one moment that only lifeforms that you are familiar with; humans, animals and plants are all that the dimensions contain.

We cannot and will not describe the totality of life in the dimensions. Some, you would have difficulty in accepting, some would be frightening to you and some would amaze you. It will suffice, for the purpose of this book, to investigate just those life forms that are interested in planet earth and its biodiversity and that manifest here from time to time.

Let us now devote this chapter to the investigation of a dimension.

For the sake of honesty, we must state that what we are going to explain is true but, will be only a minute fraction of the totality of a dimension.

So, as we said, if we take a dimension and pull it apart (if such a thing was possible), we would see a vast number of frequencies - a subset of light - each frequency slightly different from its neighbour.

There would be an incalculable number of these frequencies, each one using a distinct and separate frequency to any other frequency but, eventually, the whole series of these frequencies, contained within a coating of thick gravity to keep these frequencies separate but together, and we call that a dimension.

The question is, why do we need so many sub-frequencies in a dimension?

We have already partly answered that question in previous works and have explained that each dimension is multitasking and deals with the manipulation of life in various aspects.

So, it must be obvious that we would need more than one band to deal with a multitude of different events.

Now, we wish to say something at this point that, as far as we are aware, has never been revealed to the public and it is this.

You may remember us telling you in book four, that in this galaxy sized sphere, every molecule of life that would ever be needed was created. Countless, countless molecules of life.

Well, those molecules needed to go somewhere when they transferred to our galaxy, as we have explained in previous books.

So, the extraordinary thing that was created by the Archangels was a sub-frequency, a sub-dimension, for each and every one of these molecules and so each molecule, with its own particular, unique frequency, is placed in a unique sub-frequency of the same frequency of any particular molecule.

Now, that is a mouthful to digest, so let us explain that again.

Let us use a simple example. Imagine that there were only 10 molecules, each one vibrating at a unique frequency (1Hz, 2Hz, 3Hz, etc).

Now imagine that each molecule was placed within or on its relevant sub-frequency, also vibrating at 1Hz, 2Hz, 3Hz and so on...

So, now we would have a dimension consisting of 10 sub-dimensions and each one containing a molecule and each sub-dimension vibrating at the same frequency as it's molecule.

Then that dimension was itself made to vibrate at a different frequency to any of the sub frequencies. Can you understand that simple analogy? We hope so because we wish to explain further.

We have already said that you, for example, are actually an eight-fold person. There is what you consider to be your physical body and then there are seven other versions of you in other dimensions.

So, you are a person with eight bodies and each body corresponds to the frequency of one of the eight dimensions.

So, if there were 10 molecules and those 10 molecules were connected to 10 sub-dimensions of a particular dimension, then it was all repeated seven times more, each molecule being an eight-fold aspect of life and each molecule connected to a different dimension. Already this is becoming somewhat unwieldy.

But now, just try to imagine the reality. All of these countless molecules that we mentioned are actually eight-fold entities, and each aspect vibrates at a different frequency to any other aspect of the same molecule.

So, now we have a molecule of life on a sub-frequency of a dimension and that is repeated eight times, connected to the eight dimensions but all of different vibrations.

But, what is difficult to visualise, is the vast number of molecules, each one vibrating at a particular frequency and each one repeated eight times and placed on one of the eight dimensions.

Thus, we will say again, so as to make the concept perfectly clear.
There are countless molecules that were created long ago, enough molecules of all sorts to cover the needs of creation from the dawns of time, until it all ends far into the future.
Each one of these molecules is actually eight molecules, each version of the same molecule vibrating at a slightly different frequency.
Then, for every molecule, a band, a sub-dimension is created in each of the eight dimensions and each one of these bands vibrates to the same frequency as the frequency of one of the eight molecules.
So, each molecule is placed on its respective band or frequency – sub-dimension - in its respective main dimension.

Then we hope you can see that a molecule of something is placed on each of the eight main dimensions and each one of these molecules has its own unique sub-frequency to enable it to advance both together and in an individual fashion, throughout its development.

So, to hammer the point home, if we may cite you as an example, you are made of countless molecules of life and have, actually, eight bodies, each one of a different frequency and each one placed in one of the dimensions.
The reason that you think you are on this dimension, is because you have your focus on this dimension. But you could, if you wished, learn to turn your focus onto any of the other seven versions of you, and you would visit and experience the world's that have been created overtime by other beings, who have developed a different version of reality in the other seven dimensions.

Now, we need to understand the way life develops.
We have mentioned the countless molecules and have said that each one has eight separate forms of existence.

Now, we have also said that a molecule might be almost any element; oxygen, hydrogen, and on and on through the periodic table, including ones that science has not yet confirmed.

But a molecule of oxygen, say, is not much use on its own. It is alive but cannot actually do much. So, molecules start to combine, under the guidance of the Archangels, to form more sentient creatures. Over time they might become almost anything; animal, vegetable, mineral, human or alien.

As we have explained, each molecule will be stamped with a Logos, that not only tells it that it is going to be, say, a horse, but will belong exclusively to that particular horse. The same applies to every human. When molecules are encouraged to come together to form a human, each molecule is stamped with the Logos that tells it that it is going to help form a human but also tells it that it must always remain with a certain human. That human might be you, me or anyone else but each molecule, once it has been given the Logos by the Archangels, knows that it is going to be part of one specific human.

This is all very well but we mentioned that each molecule was repeated eight times. So, while the molecules are coming together on one dimension to form a human - in the astral worlds, of course - what is happening to its other seven versions of each molecule?

The answer is that they, too, are encouraged to form a human that will greatly resemble you but in seven other dimensions.
So, after a certain time, a human is formed in the astral planes from all the molecules but repeated eight times in all, the main difference being, that they are all in different dimensions, made of different vibrations. But, they will also be linked to you by an aspect of the Logos that tells each version of you that it must remain linked with you throughout all time.
So, when you look at yourself in a mirror, if you could see with psychic eyes, would see seven more versions of you, attached to you. We call them auras and we have explained all that in a previous book.
Thus, you are an eight-fold person. You have your focus on this one version of you at the moment but you could, as we have said, transfer your attention into any one of your other seven bodies and experience life from that point of view.
It takes training, of course, but is possible to do.

We will end this chapter here, although we will say that we have only scratched the surface of the subject of dimensions in this chapter.
We explained more fully in the book on auras, which is just another name for dimensions.

The main point we wish you to retain from this rather difficult chapter, is that every molecule, every atom of all creation, has its own unique place created in a dimension and that each molecule is repeated eight times in all and each version of that molecule has its own place created in each one of the eight dimensions.

These eight molecules retain a link with each other and largely progress together until asked to create a 'something' and that something will be created eight times, each version being of a slightly different vibration but linked together as one object but with seven auras.
This applies to everything everywhere in the universe. Eight versions linked as one.

CHAPTER 2

PERSONALITIES

So, we progress with this analysis of how life is placed into the dimensions and encouraged to grow and develop in an eight-fold manner, but each version, in principle, closely connected, and we could say that they are reflections of each other.

We will say that each person, animal, plant or mineral that is in your reality, has what looks like a physical form and seven auras.

But, if one were to transfer one's consciousness into one of the auras, that would appear to be a solid object standing on a solid planet and the so-called physical body that you have now, would be seen as an aura.

Thus, we hope you can realise that physicality is actually an astral form that appears solid, but should you move to another of your bodies, this world would be seen for what it is, just one of the eight versions of life, each of them appearing solid when we are using our consciousness to focus upon anyone of them, but they are all, in fact, just auric matter.

It is our focus, our consciousness, that gives each aura apparent solidity.

This is an important point to understand and, at the risk of appearing to labour the point, we would like to explore and expand on that concept.

We mentioned in chapter one that all life was placed in sub-dimensions of an aura (dimension) and each particle of life was repeated eight times, in eight subdivisions of eight dimensions.

Each one of these elements was given a stamp, a Logos, which is a sort of list of information for each element of life that tells it a number of things to which it has to concord.

The object must become part of a 'something'. Let us say, to demonstrate the point, to become a human although it could have been anything.

So, the Logos would tell all eight versions of every element a human would need, that they are destined to become one version - of eight - of a human.

Further, those many elements, atoms, particles of everything a human needs, are informed that they will become a particular human.

So, strange as it may seem, to consider you, long before you were actually formed, long before you were even a twinkle in your father's eye, if you understand what we mean, the elements that eventually became you, were instructed to make you.

So, you would not be born in a haphazard fashion.

You were destined to be who you are long, long before you had any idea that you existed.

This is an impressive thing to realise. Many, many long years ago, the Archangels decided to create you and all the countless elements of all sorts that you need to 'be', both physical and astral, were told to come together to create you.

Further, of course, there are eight versions of you so, this vast number of elements needed to create you, was repeated in all of the eight dimensions and, truly, countless atoms - in astral form - leapt into action and came together to create you eight times.

Each one of these atoms, these elements, these particles of life, were instructed not only to create a human but, specifically, to create you. Exclusively you and no one else.

That is why, even now, with every breath you take, with every bit of food you eat, with every drop of water you drink, only the elements that have your stamp on them are absorbed into your body, the rest being eliminated as waste when you need to evacuate your intestines or bladder. In other terms, when you feel the need to visit the bathroom.

Can you fully appreciate this marvel?

Long, long ago, a sufficient number of molecules were given your unique stamp, not only to form you but still, here on Earth, there are elements with your stamp on them, either floating in the air, contained in plants or even in the bodies of animals, to satisfy the needs of your body. Just to keep you alive.

And all this is repeated eight times.

However, it must be said that in the astral spheres, these elements that are taking care of your other seven bodies, can be drawn directly from the cosmic forces and there is no need to visit the bathroom.

Your other seven bodies ingest just what is needed for you and no more.

It is only in physicality that elements, that would be required by others, are ingested with the food and drink that you put into your body and all those elements not required by your body are eliminated and will, ultimately, find their way to their correct destination, no matter what that might be.

It would be good if we could ingest just those elements required by our physical body but, in fact, the physical bodies of sentient creatures - humans included - are designed to process food and drink, and to deprive those organs of doing their job would create illness. So, all sentient beings are designed to digest food and liquid and extract the elements that correspond to that entity and reject the rest.

We hope that you can understand that the Archangels that decided to create you, caused all the elements that you needed to be formed in the astral worlds and even here in incarnation, to vibrate to one, unique frequency.

Thus, you, who are reading this book, are vibrating at a particular, unique frequency, as are all the elements waiting to be ingested by you.

All are already vibrating at your frequency and will only ever be attracted to you.

In the meantime, your other seven bodies which are in other dimensions, vibrate to different frequencies but that are unique to you.

But now, if all these different bodies, which were created independently on the 8 dimensions, are all vibrating at different frequencies, what is the glue that attaches them all together to create one, eightfold person, rather like creating a small book of eight pages but these eight pages being connected to make one book?

The answer, we must say, is gravity.

If you can imagine this, you, as you go about on planet Earth, apparently as a single person, have with you all the time, seven more auras that are in astral form but, generally, invisible to your eyes and senses.

But, all these other seven bodies are permanently attached to you by a form of gravity, that ensures that these other bodies are always with you.

We wish to explain and emphasize that we use the term, not quite in the sense of the gravity that we explained in another book, almost a form of magnetism. It is not that. We used the word gravity because we have no other word that describes what is occurring.

The various other seven bodies that are attached to you, is due to a form of consciousness. Even that is not quite accurate. This will be a new concept for mankind incarnate, so words do not exist to describe the force, the desire, the sense of attachment that links all your auras - your other bodies - to you.

Imagine a small child, a girl who has seven dolls to which she is very attached, very fond of.

She might try to carry them about with her, pretend to feed them, sleep with them and, in a way, they become part of her and, should one vanish for whatever reason, she would be most upset.

We could call it love, but love is such a strong word in all its ramifications that the child's small level of comprehension could not possibly fully grasp the concept of cosmic love.

But, she is deeply attached to her seven dolls and cares for the every - imagined - need as if they were alive. To her they are alive and she might well have names and she might invent personalities for each doll.

She would praise them if they were good and scold them if they were naughty.

Now, we created that small but charming scenario to try to describe the attachment that you have with your seven auras and they have for you.

There is no physical attachment and any aura could wander off at will at any time but they don't.

They remain in close, if invisible, contact with you due to this emotion very much like the child has for her dolls.

It is a form of love, but that would not be correct.

We could call it a sense of friendship but that would not be right.

It is as if a sort of group unity forms between the child and her dolls and it is this form of unity that keeps your auras, your other seven bodies attached to you.

We could call it a form of gravity and, in a way, it is so, but it is a much more spiritual, loving force than we imagine when we think of gravity.

Gravity seems a cold magnetic force, the sort of thing a scientist or mathematician might talk about.

We would have difficulty in imagining a mathematician describing in mathematical form the love that a child would have for her dolls.

But, it is that love that keeps all your seven auric bodies attached to you.

This love is the sort of emotional connection that we hope man will develop as he advances spiritually.

Jesus said, 'love thy neighbour as yourself'. Now, not all people love themselves but we hope that, one day, all people will learn to love themselves and, eventually love all life in whatever form it takes. The word neighbour is a mistranslation. Jesus was trying to say love everything as that child loves her dolls and as your auras love you. Then mankind will start really to comprehend that all is one.

The problem, as we said, is that a word does not exist to describe deep affection that we can have for each other. It is love but it is a different form of the word love.

So, to go back to any person, animal, vegetable matter or mineral, no matter how big or how small, there are always, no matter what medium that object lives in - physical or astral - a focus point and 7 other versions of that same object, each one standing on a planet corresponding to the frequency of that dimension.

This is a very important point that must clearly be understood by any student of cosmic consciousness.

There are many people who are under the impression that the only planet with any solidity is planet Earth and that the auras that surround us are just some pretty lights that one strives to visualise but this is not true at all.

We are all eightfold beings and each one of our bodies, although seen as coloured lights surrounding our body when we are focused on Earth, is in fact a solid body standing on a solid planet.

It is just the difference in frequency that enables them to be seen as coloured light.

If a person was to transfer his focus from his Earthly vehicle to one of his auras, the Earthly body would be seen as a coloured light surrounding whatever body he was using at the time.

While we are discussing these bodies, these auras, it is worth discussing also which form of controlling energy governs the focus of these bodies.

By that we mean that, when one is incarnate and is living on planet Earth, we have mentioned all the various aspects, the Higher Self, Imagination, ID and so on, that goes into making a person incarnate.

But, should we be focused in or on one of our other bodies, from whence comes all the controlling elements that would make it operate in as good a fashion as the Earthly body?

For instance, when an incarnation comes to an end and the person returns to his heavenly home, he appears to be still using all the spiritual parts; Higher Self, Imagination, etc., that he used on Earth, because he is the same person but minus his physical body. So, effectively, there would be no change and he would still have his other seven bodies (auras) attached to him.

But what if he transfers his attention into one of his other bodies, one of his auras? What happens?

The answer is quite simple, in that whatever aura is being activated, that one becomes the controlling body and the others are seen as auras.

All that goes into making a living, thinking person on Earth, simply transfers to the appropriate active body and all the rest we call auras just attach themselves to the activated body.

So, with very limited exceptions, there is only one body active at a time, the others all being inactive and so there is only need for one actual consciousness controlling the active body, the other bodies being asleep - if one may use such a feeble word.

But, if we think about this for a moment, it indicates that what we referred to as consciousness is independent, outside of any of our bodies.
We have talked about this in other works and have stated that there is actually only one consciousness for all beings.
We appear to have our own versions of everything; Higher Self, Imagination, ID and so on but, in fact, there is only one of it all and we just share - thanks to our own sense of being alive - aspects of that one consciousness.

So, to put the lid on all this, we want you clearly to realise that you have eight very similar bodies, each one only separated from the others by being of a different frequency and none of these bodies has any form of life outside of the one set of aspects of life that all share, but that we all use to give meaning to our existence in general and our personal aspects of existence in particular.

It is of vital importance to realise this.
Thus, we will repeat it again and, if necessary, we will repeat it endlessly until you have understood.
You are an eight-fold being, with eight bodies standing on eight planets.
None of your bodies are alive outside of the spirit forces that appear to animate whichever one your attention is focused in.
There is only one consciousness for all of us, past, present or future.
But, to enable you to have some form of independent life, you have the ability to contact, to interact with that one consciousness, as if it were your own and thus move, think, act as if you had an independent life force of your own, exclusive to you.

But you - from a spiritual aspect - are part and parcel of every other person, because there is only one consciousness, one Higher Self, one Imagination, one ID.
That is why we are all one.

We apologise for endlessly labouring this point but there are so many people throughout both the world and throughout time that have not realised this very important point. It has been taught by most religions that we are all separate entities - usually with the implication that only those belonging to a particular religion would be saved, the rest going to hell - and that idea of separation has been at the base of most of the wars and conflicts that have rocked the world since man first walked the Earth.
For peace to reign, this concept must be eliminated, replaced with the simple truth that we are all one.

But, let us return to the subject of this particular chapter, which was a continuation of the elements revealed in chapter one, a study of the countless elements, particles, atoms if you will and the fact that each one is repeated eight times and placed on one of the sub-dimensions of the eight main dimensions.

We have never really explained why God, in conjunction with his Archangels, decided to create eight main dimensions and, to be honest, it is not only outside of the purview of this book but we, ourselves, do not know for sure.
There is nothing magical about the number eight, any more than there is about any other number.
For all we know, there might be more dimensions about which we have never heard.
But we know of eight main dimensions, carrier waves if you prefer, each one containing the number of sub-dimensions, one for each particle in existence and each dimension containing 1/8th of the totality of each element.
As we said, why it was chosen rather than any other number is not our concern. We analyse what exists and do not speculate on what might exist or might have existed.

Now, we must try, before this book can really deal with the topics of the various beings that live in and on the multitude of subdimensions, deal with why anyone or anything would require more than one astral body. Why eight?
The answer, as always, can be made to appear complex but is actually quite simple when one understands.
All life, no matter what it is and where it appears to live, is too complex for the totality of it to be contained within one entity.
If you think just about yourself, for instance, you must realise that you have a number of aspects to you that might appear somewhat contradictory.
We will give one simple example that we have mentioned before and it concerns mainly females, animal or human.
In the case of a human female, when she is young, unattached to a man, she will do her best, at all times when she is in public, to appear as best as she can.
She will take great interest in her physical appearance; makeup, hairstyle, keeping her body shape what she hopes is as attractive as possible, choosing her clothes with great care.
She will at all times try, in social events, to put her best foot forward, and try to appear witty, joyful, etc. The whole object, whether she realises it or not, is to attract a male with whom she can procreate.
Obviously, there are exceptions, but, in general, that is what is happening.
Once she has attracted a suitable male, generally, at some point she turns her attention to creating a family. Thus, by accident or design she attempts to become pregnant.

Now, from what we have described there is at least one aspect that is driving the lady: ego. She wants to stand out from the crowd and attract a mate. She may not call it ego, indeed, she may never really stop to consider what is driving her, but let's call it ego.
So, it would make sense to have amongst the eight bodies, one of which is connected to the concept, the emotion of ego.

Now, we realise that this is probably not all that drives the female, but we can say that she has one body, the main focus of which is ego.

Now, we assume that she has become pregnant and, up to a point, she proudly shows off with special clothing that she is 'with child'. Ego is still playing its part.

But, eventually, baby is born and although the mother is still proud of her achievement - ego - another element kicks in, and that we call motherly love. She put herself, her desires, her wants and needs second and puts the child first.
So, we could say that another body is activated - one of maternal love.
Now we have two of the eight bodies (auras) active: ego and maternal love.

Obviously, there will be a conflict going on as to which of the two bodies - ego and maternal love - takes precedence.
The lady wants to regain her former beauty as quickly as possible - ego -, but, at the same time she has to devote a large amount of time to caring for her baby - motherly love.
We will leave the lady to battle with her opposing influences and turn our attention to examining other aspects of personality manifest in what we called the astral bodies.

Now, it must be obvious, that at first glance several things have come to light.
The first is that these eight bodies we mentioned, one on each of the dimensions, are not actually bodies as we would imagine them to be in physicality. We used the term bodies to help explain that life, all life, is eightfold.
There is a form of creation, an aspect of a person, animal, plant or mineral on each of the eight dimensions and it was easier to explain them as bodies.
But, in reality they are aspects of personality.
We will just say at this point that it is difficult to imagine a grain of sand as having a personality but, as all is one, it has these eight aspects attached to it although they are dormant at the moment.

But, us humans are rather more evolved and so access to our aspects of personality are more easily obtained.
These aspects would include; love, hate, ego (as we have mentioned), maternal instinct, desire to create art, desire to investigate science/mathematics and so on.

Now, there are more than eight aspects of personality but most of them are subsets of the basic personality points.
Also, we must say that, according to the way the person developed in the heavenly spheres, and according to his life plan, he would have certain aspects more developed than others.
So, into each of the eight dimensions, is placed one of eight of a person's basic emotions or personality aspects. Each of these aspects of personality have a similar power at first. That is to say that no one aspect is more prominent than another - with the exception of one - ego.

A baby, to survive, must have its ego strongly developed. It cares only for itself. When it is hungry, thirsty, in pain or in any way uncomfortable, it lets the mother know by screaming at the top of its voice for that need or desire to be fulfilled.

What is interesting, is that in later life, there are a number of people who grow to adulthood, with that childish ego still very much in the forefront of their personality. We have all seen people who go through their life looking after themselves, their wants and needs, both real and imagined, to the exclusion of anyone else.
They have, in a fact, never grown up.
Equally, there are people who allow hate or fear to dominate their existence.

The point we are making is that all these different 'bodies', placed on the various dimensions, are aspects of personality, that one can pull forward or push back to influence the person, rather as if the person was remote from and separate from his aspects of personality.
Investigation of this aspect will be the subject of the next chapter.

CHAPTER 3

ROCKS

We have attempted so far in this book, to explain the strange truth that we are all just one person - although we must say, for the sake of honesty, that even this is not completely true.

In reality, the only thing that exists is consciousness.

Now, consciousness is a concept that is truly difficult to imagine and only the very wisest Archangels really understand just what it is.

The rest of us just have to live with a limited understanding of the meaning of it, so there is no use in us going into a long and, no doubt, meaningless explanation of consciousness.

It would make more sense at this stage of our development to accept that we are all one aspect of existence, all one person and leave it at that.

That concept is already difficult to appreciate and, no doubt, there will be many who will reject it.

However, to repeat what we have already said, we are in fact - from this point of view - just one person but, thanks to our eight aspects of personality, housed on each of the eight dimensions, we can all consider ourselves to be individuals.

We hope you can visualise this. You have eight aspects of personality, housed one on each of the eight dimensions and so does absolutely everything else.

Every human has eight aspects of personality attached exclusively to him. Every animal, plant or mineral also has eight aspects of personality attached to him (it), as does every other entity anywhere in existence.

That simple phrase has far reaching consequences. Who amongst you has any real idea of the outreach of existence?

Most people have some idea about some of the billions of humans alive at the moment on Earth, although there exist groups of humans that live apart from the rest of you and, very possibly, of whom you have no awareness.

Then, some of you have some idea of the myriad of animals roaming the fields, forests, seas and lakes. But not one of you has a complete knowledge.

Some of you may be aware of the various types of rock that exist.

Some may have heard of aliens, seen spaceships in the skies. Some may claim to have interacted with certain races but who amongst you could honestly stand up and say that he knows every facet of existence?

Most, truly, have little more knowledge, factual knowledge, about life than the average caveman had many thousands of years ago.

It is mostly conjecture based on false interpretation of the evidence.

The problem has always been, for the general public, that they have been taught to look at the entities roaming Earth and consider that is all that exists. As we have attempted to explain in the various works we have presented to you, we are looking down the wrong end of the telescope. That which is observable to the naked eye, is just the end result of a long process that started vast amounts of time in the past and in the remotest corners of creation.

We hope that you lucky few, that have access to our teachings will, at last, be able to have some idea of the complexity and wonders of creation.

These teachings will of course spread with time and with the efforts of all those involved in the dissemination of this wisdom and will contribute greatly to the advance of mankind.

But now let us return to the rather intricate subject of the various dimensions, the personalities contained within them, and start to look at the complexity of life contained within those personalities.

You must, at all times, understand that there is only one consciousness, so no matter what we describe to you, all are connected to you and are, in a way, you.

It is only the different personalities that the Archangels endowed each and every entity with that gives it the appearance of remoteness from you.

Having repeated that information, ad nauseam, we will begin to describe the different aspects of creation and take the time to examine each one as clearly as possible in order to make this book an encyclopedia in its own right, to which people may turn if questioning any aspect of life.

So where shall we begin?

As this chapter is so short, let us begin with an aspect that will not take many pages to describe because there is not much to talk about.

Let us begin by examining mineral life; sand, rocks, crystals and the other elements that fit into the mineral department.

Now, if you have ever visited a geological museum, you may have been amazed at the corridors of exhibits of all sorts and types but, if you were really to examine them, you would find that a stone from Britain and a stone from Sumatra, really is very largely the same in general appearance and scarcely warrants to be proudly put on display like some circus act!

But, what interests us is not the physical appearance of the stones but what is going on spiritually - non-physical would be a better term.

Like all things, every element (molecule) that constitutes any stone, large or small, or any mountain, was created long ago in that giant atom looking object that we described in a previous book.

So, the stone will follow the same development, as does all things.

However, even though the stone has eight channels or places created for it in the eight dimensions, it hardly needs acute aspects of its personality developed to exist.

So, what aspects of personality would a stone need to exist?

The first thing we need to remind you about, in case you have either forgotten or are unaware, is that each and every mineral has a unique frequency. No matter if it is a grain of sand or a mountain, it has a unique frequency.

This has been made use of throughout the world to create huge monuments, broadcasting a frequency into the skies which enables some space faring nations to navigate either towards Earth or around Earth.

This unique frequency is part of the basic makeup of a stone and was given that frequency at the moment of its creation long, long ago.

So, we wish you to comprehend that when you leave a city and walk in the countryside, each and every grain of sand, each stone, no matter how large or small, each mountain, is broadcasting (projecting) outwards for a greater or lesser distance, vibrations. For those who have psychic eyesight developed, these stones would be projecting light of various colours and the whole of planet Earth scintillates with light.

The reason that this is so, is simple. Everything is vibration and is a subset of starlight (pure white light).

The various personality channels that each mineral object has in the eight dimensions, are also vibrating at the same frequency as each piece of mineral, and thus are also glowing to the frequency of the object being observed.

Thus, it is surrounded by the glow of the dimensional auras, which surround each and every piece of mineral.

Now, believe it or not, some minerals are more alive than others. This is not so strange as it seems. Crystals are attributed to having special powers.

These powers would also be a form of vibration, and thus if a crystal is alive enough to have special powers, it would draw advanced forms of personality towards it compared to other forms of rock containing no crystal elements in its construction.

Thus, we hope that you can appreciate that each type of rock, not only has a unique vibration but also has a degree of awareness, not only its basic awareness that it exists but, depending on the type of rock, it has a specific degree of other attributes.

It is worth mentioning at this point that crystals should be treated with the greatest circumspection.

Depending on the type of crystal, and depending on its size, a crystal might generate a great deal of force, some of these forces being inimical to man.

Many years ago, the sages understood crystals and harvested their powers for various reasons. But, today, they are often considered pretty ornaments and people collect them to beautify their homes rather as if they were bouquets of flowers. This is an error.

Equally, people buy crystals from sellers, who make claims as to the aid a particular crystal might give; helping with health, finance, beauty, love life, etc.

Once again, all this is an error. The influence of crystals has no connection to the above human considerations. Crystals are quite independent and separate from any human wants or needs.

Their powers lie in different directions than beautifying a home or helping solve human problems. Thus, it would be better for the average person to avoid collecting crystals. Some of them are actually harmful to man and can generate all sorts of health problems, physical or emotional.

Years ago, their powers were harvested to generate forces, in what would be called magic ceremonies, because their powers were understood. They were never used as modern man uses them.

We should also mention that planet Earth contains a great deal of rock, sub-terrain or under the seas. This huge mass of rock, generally, has one unique vibration and equates to the frequency that the Earth sends out to space, and to the sun, and contributes to the gravitational effect that holds the Earth in orbit around the sun.

So, there is not a lot more to say about rocks generally. Whilst they play a fundamental and vital role on Earth, forming not only the quasi totality of planet Earth, but also is largely responsible for helping hold the planet in orbit around the sun.

But, from the point of view of consideration of personalities, apart from crystals that we have mentioned, rocks do not generate much energy.

So, let us go on to consider plants.

CHAPTER 4

THE PLANT KINGDOM

We looked in the last chapter at stones, rocks, mountains and crystals and came to the conclusion that, although each of those objects had unique frequencies and aspects of personality placed within the eight dimensions, with the exception of crystals, they could hardly be described as having personalities.

However, when we investigate plants; grasses, vegetation of various types and trees, we can see a much more advanced form of life.
Once again, we must stress that each little grass plant, vegetable, flower, bush or tree has a unique frequency and each one has its aspects of personality placed in the eight dimensions.

Clearly, however, we can also see that each vegetable object is much more alive than a stone and we must be aware that each object in the vegetable realm knows that it is alive and does its best to succeed in growing, even at the expense of stifling the growth of other objects growing close to it.
We have explained the reason why in other books.
This drive to succeed at all costs is the ego part of the plant, helping the God force contained within the plant to be dominant.
So, we can guess that, amongst the various personality aspects present in the eight dimensions, ego will be very prominent.

Now, there is a vast range to the vegetable realm, from tiny plants to mighty trees and each one is aware, from the very beginning of its creation, exactly what it is destined to become.
So, we can say, that amongst the eight aspects of personality, is its knowledge of exactly what each plant will become. There is an interesting aspect of most vegetation in that, in a way, it has two aspects to its life force. First, it has the knowledge that it is alive and second, it has the knowledge of what it is destined to become.

Most plants start off as seeds, some small and some quite large. We will look inside a seed to see what is going on later but let us assume for now that a seed is alive and knows that it is alive. It is just awaiting the moment when conditions are right for that life force to spring forth from the seed.
So, the seed is planted in Earth and watered, either by man or by nature.
Then, something amazing occurs. The plant puts forth two leaves. The thing is that amongst virtually all plants, these first two leaves are more or less identical. Some might be larger than others but a gardener would have great difficulty in describing exactly what plant was going to be produced just by looking at the first pair of leaves - they all look the same.
It is not until the second pair of leaves are produced that the plant can be named.

The reason for this is easy to understand.

Assuming that the seed is alive, that initial life force is the God force that springs from the seed. As God does not create personalities - God just creates life - the plant does not actually know at that point what it is going to be. It just knows that it is a plant and alive, so it puts out a pair of leaves to draw light into the seed to help with the growth process.

But, that seed also has eight possible personality aspects and it is one of those that knows just what the plant is going to be.

The personality aspects, contained within the dimensions (auras), associate with the plant shortly after the seed bursts into life.

It is similar with the personality system that links with a human baby at the moment of birth.

But seed, or baby, has life first and personalities (auras) second.

So, in the case of a plant, the life force contained in association with the seed, as it springs to life, helps push out two leaves, then the auras surround the plant and its designation links; geranium, oak tree or whatever.

Only then do leaves start to grow that can be recognised by a gardener.

Once again, we return to the aspects of personality that we mentioned in relation to stones.

At the risk of repeating ourselves we need to reinforce the concept that each and every plant has eight possible personality traits, one on each of the various dimensions or auras.

We have already stated that first and foremost amongst plants is what we might call ego. This is really the God force striving to survive at all costs.

Therefore, if we could see surrounding the plant, it's auras, we would see, shining the most forcefully, that which corresponds to the desire to survive at all costs - ego.

However, depending on the type of plant, some are much more developed than others.

For example, a mighty oak, or the sort of tree capable of surviving for thousands of years, although it would not have awareness compared to humans, nevertheless, for those who have psychic vision they would sense that a tree can be much more alive than some basic plants.

It would be instructive to try to analyse some of these aspects of life, of awareness.

Therefore, we can understand that the plant knows that it is alive, so the question is, is that awareness one of the aspects of personality, or is it just the awareness that all life might have been created by God?

We can tell you that it is an aspect of personality.

Not all things know that they are alive. Indeed, there are many basic elements of existence that do not have that awareness.

We might well assume that molecules of substances like oxygen, hydrogen, etc., although alive, do not actually have awareness that they are alive, although they are very much alive and form the basic ingredients of virtually all life.

If it were not for molecules of all types, life as we know it in any and all dimensions could not exist but, taken individually, none of them have sufficient awareness to know that they are alive.

It is only when they come together to form a "something", that something can realise that it is alive.

As we are examining plants, let us consider that all plants, from the tiniest to the greatest, have an aspect of personality sufficiently developed so as to know that it is alive.

May we at this point say that we are using the word "plants" to cover all aspects of flora, as the word flora may not be known to all English speaking people, whereas plants is a word more generally known.
But, we wish you to comprehend, that when we speak of plants, we include everything that exists in the flora kingdom. Not only flowering plants but shrubs, bushes, trees, and everything that contains vegetable matter.

So, to return to the consideration of plants and the aspects of personality.
We already mentioned ego and said that it was the most powerful, prominent aspect of personality.
Most things that can move; animals, humans and so on have the fight/flight aspect fairly well developed. This is an aspect of ego, the desire to survive at all costs. This desire to survive is, as we have mentioned, the God force pushing the creature to live long enough to procreate, thus assuring the continuation of its species.

However, the vast majority of plants cannot move. There are a few exceptions, mainly in aquatic species but even they tend to just float about at the mercy of wind and tide.
So, flight is not really an option in the plant kingdom. But fight is and most plants, once they have sufficiently grown, as to allow their personalities (auras) to join them, can put up a pretty good show at defending themselves.
Some grow to become powerful solo objects.
Some develop into large clumps that we call bushes, while others develop sharp spines (thorns) to prevent animals from eating them.
Then, of course, many have developed poisonous toxins in sap, leaves or stems that discourage from being consumed.
Modern and ancient medicine, has found numerous uses for these toxins and it is fair to say that medicine as we know it would not be, if it were not for the toxins that plants have developed over time.

Although many plants prove beneficial to both mankind and to animals, we must stress that the primary aim of the plants in developing these molecules, so helpful to medicine, was and is, to discourage people and animals from consuming them.

So, all this development; size, thorns, toxins, came about as a result of ego.
And ego, as we have said, is the result of the God force pushing the plant to survive at all costs. It is the fight aspect of fight/flight used by mobile creatures.

Therefore, we now have two aspects of personality active; awareness of being alive and ego.
A moment's thought would reveal that these two aspects are closely connected and could be considered to be one. If the plant knows that it is alive, it follows that it will have the desire to survive until it has the chance to procreate in order to further its species. But, in fact they are separate.

Whilst it is true that, once a plant knows that it is alive, it naturally has the desire to survive at all costs, this is not always the case with all creatures.

We have mentioned the example of creatures, or beings that will sacrifice their lives to protect their young and, with reluctance, we must mention the few misguided humans who reject the gift of life and commit suicide.

Although these two examples are at opposite ends of the scale in terms of courage, one giving its life to enable others to survive and the other not having the courage to face life, the result is the same, a conscious life force losing its Earthly incarnation.

However, in the case of plants, this does not happen.

A plant will not sacrifice itself to save another, nor would it end its life through cowardice.

Plants cling to life as long as they can, as long as their life plan enables them so to do.

So, we consider ego and the knowledge of life as two independent aspects of personality.

Let us go on and examine other parts of personality of plants.

The next one would be the desire to be in a position to procreate.

Virtually all plants procreate through pollination although, of course, other methods are also used.

Pollination is, of course, closely related to methods of sexual fertilization used by creatures able to move; mammals, reptiles, etc.

There might be botanists who would not entirely agree but their lack of vision is not our concern.

Although there are various methods of producing offspring, many plants use the following system.

A plant will produce an organ that acts rather as a phallus does in more animate entities.

Either the same plant or one of the same species will produce the ability to act as a female.

Then pollen acts rather as sperm does in mobile creatures.

Obviously, this is a generalization but we hope that the student can see the similarity between the way plants and more sentient creatures reproduce.

The main difference is that, in the case of mobile creatures, they are able to meet in order to procreate whereas, in the case of plants, being static, some other system must be employed in order to transfer the sperm of the male to the vagina of the female plant.

This might be air currents - wind - or it might be flying insects.

The idea is that a male and female of the same or similar species join to create the next generation.

Then, of course, seeds are formed which contain that next generation.

We give this brief and incomplete lesson in plant biology in order to bring to your attention another aspect of plant personality, sex drive. The desire to mate and further the next generation of that plant family.

So, the list of personality aspects is growing.

We have ego, knowledge of being alive, and sex drive.

What other aspects of plants could we attribute to personality in plants?

We could say that the form and beauty of the flowers of a plant are influenced by personality although, once again, botanists might not agree.

But the simple truth is that plants, long ago, discovered that certain colours, certain perfumes, attract flying insects and thus aid in pollination, whereas other colours and perfumes will repel the same creatures.

Thus, it is that plants consciously choose certain colours, certain perfumes and even certain shapes, that enable the sex act to be successfully accomplished and thus that species, that plant, to procreate more successfully.

This may just seem to be a reflection of the "survival of the fittest" concept but it is, in fact, a conscious desire of the plant in question to appear dressed in his or her finest clothes to attract suitable insects to aid in pollination - fertilisation.

This aspect of personality we might call dress sense, not a very good scientific name, but we are interested in helping you understand the mindset of a plant, not writing a biological treatise.

You may have noticed a link between the aspects of personality we have so far described. Dress sense links to sex drive, which also links to ego which, in turn, is linked to awareness of being alive.

Life implies reproduction and, although in the plant kingdom there are a number of forms of reproduction, if one gazes over a field in the countryside that has been left to its own devices, nature will have covered that field with countless beautiful little flowers, each one dressed in its finery to attract passing insects, to aid each plant in its effort to reproduce.

But there is yet another aspect that we must consider. Anyone who has had the opportunity, the great pleasure to gaze over a field that has been left abandoned for some years and has had the opportunity to allow nature to clothe it, will have noticed the vast number of different plants, different species, all growing intermingled in a seemingly haphazard fashion.

Then, countless insects will be observed gathering pollen and, unwittingly, fluttering from flower to flower, depositing male pollen in any number of female flowers of diverse species.

Except for very rare occasions, the sperm from one species of flower will only mix and mate with the ova of the same species. All other accidental attempts to fertilise will be fruitless (wasted).

So, it is obvious that each plant and each family of plants is aware when it is being mated with some plant of his own species or of a species not compatible with it.

This, strange as it may seem, is part of personality.

In a way we could call plants "racist", in that they tend to mate only with their own kind, although, of course, the plants do not think like that and we use that rather offensive word "racist" merely to explain that plants, generally, tend to procreate with only their own species.

So, we have yet another aspect of personality that, to keep it simple, we will term racism, although, as we said, we do not mean that term in the offensive way that it is used today. We just mean that life tends to interrelate with its own species.

So, how far have we got with aspects of personality?
* We have knowledge of life.
* Ego - the desire to survive at all costs.
* Destination - the knowledge of what it is going to be.
* Sex drive - the desire to procreate.
* Dress sense - the knowledge of how to attract insects to aid in pollination.
* Racism - the desire to stay within its own species.

No doubt we could go on and discover ever more aspects of personality but we have described six major ones and that will give some idea of the makeup of the plant kingdom.
If we were really to dive into more complex areas concerning plants, we would, perhaps, find that many other aspects; shape of leaf, shape of flower, type of perfume emitted, really are subsets of one or more of the basic personality aspects of plants.
We will also stress that we have generalized in our consideration of plants and are perfectly aware that not all plants follow the descriptions that we stated above.
We are aware that not all plants create flowers, not all create perfumes, etc., but what we have attempted to do is to explain the personality traits of the plant kingdom. We have not attempted to create a comprehensive treatise on all of the plant kingdom.
Our interest is from the hidden, esoteric aspect of plants and we have tried to get you to understand that when you look upon any plant, whatever its shape, size or color, you are looking at a living, thinking being, with aspects of personality developed and we hope that from now on, you will try to appreciate that plants are not so very different from you and share many aspects of personality with you although, in the case of most humans, they would be more developed than those of the plant kingdom.

One thing that we did not mention in relation to plants is there ability to feel.
We refer to feel; touch, pain, love, hate and so on. Plants have these abilities but we did not wish to complicate this chapter too much, so we will go on to examine the next level of life and just ask you to be considerate with plants as they, too, feel much as all living things do.

CHAPTER 5

ANIMAL TRAITS

We turn our attention, with some trepidation, to animals.

We realise that this is going to be a thorny subject to broach, as the animal kingdom is vast, ranging in size from almost molecular sized creatures, to enormous ones.

We further realise that these animals have conquered land, seas and air.

Further, the history of animals can be traced back a long way into the past and that many species have become extinct over time, while new species are either being created or at least discovered throughout planet Earth.

Equally, the animal kingdom is divided by science into various groups and given complicated Latin based names by those jealous to guard what they see as their preserve - a particular branch of the animal kingdom.

So, we are sure that amongst those who are starting this chapter, are a number of people who consider themselves experts - at least to a certain degree - on a particular branch of this form of life.

We can almost feel the hairs on their heads starting to bristle as they puff themselves up with indignation over what we might suggest concerning their special preserve.

They look back at the apparent gobbledygook we spoke concerning plants and their personalities and will bluster with indignation if we dare suggest that animals, especially insects and small creatures like that, should have personalities.

We have no wish to offend or insult anyone, but as all is one, it follows that if a human has personalities, all animal life has too, and we intend to investigate the personality aspects of the animal kingdom.

As with plants, we do not intend to consider specific creatures but to present an overall, generic, picture of what some animals have developed with regard to personalities and leave it to the appreciation of the reader to apply, or not, that information to specific animals.

We will not really consider these personality traits to how they might affect their relationship to other creatures or humans, but to consider the esoteric development of the animal kingdom.

Therefore, to start, just for those who have found this chapter on animals without having read the previous chapters of this book, and other books, we will just repeat that all animals are part and parcel of all life and, if one could strip away all the personality aspects that make animals appear different from other life forms, they would all be found to be, not only the same basic creature, but one with all life - all is one.

Then, to give each animal a sense of individuality, there is a form of identity created to enable each animal to realise its individuality and, lastly, to complete the picture, each animal has a number of personality traits.

These personality traits can come forward or backwards in importance, not only depending on its individual character but also according to its species and, lastly, according to the fact that they are animals.

So, let us try to decipher some of the personality traits of animals. If we can do that, perhaps we can begin to see just how close they are to us humans and, perhaps, people start to realise that to exploit them and to eat them is not a good idea.
The mammal kingdom is so close to the human race that to eat them could, almost, be considered to be a form of cannibalism.

The first and most obvious aspect of personality has to be ego.
Ego, as you'll see as this book unfolds can almost be taken for granted.
Without ego, survival in physical form would be almost impossible although, if one thinks about it, it is somewhat self-defeating.
We all have the desire to survive at all costs and animals are no different.
There is the need to eat. Food can consist of a number of things, either animal or vegetable or a mixture according to the species. But to survive there is the constant need to eat and drink.
So, the ego of animals pushes all animals to eat. But the problem is that for one animal, who is carnivorous, to eat, some other animal has to be eaten. Obviously, the poor animal who is potential prey does not want to be eaten, so he is in a constant state of fear.
Thus, we can say that fear is another personality trait for many, indeed most, animals.
The small animals have fear in case a larger one pounces on them and even the large carnivorous beasts are in fear in case they cannot find prey to devour.
Thus, we have two aspects of personality highly developed.
1. Ego - the desire to survive
2. Fear - of not finding food or of being eaten itself.

As we have previously stated, all things are created and contain the God force. This God force pushes everything to survive as long as its life plan decrees that it should last in incarnation and also pushes it to mate to reproduce its species.
Closely related to this fear is the fight/flight reaction.
A large creature will fight, not only to survive, but fight for food and fight for the right to mate. This is the God force at work.
Although we have stated that God is love - and this is true - God also requires a kingdom to develop in order for the experiences of each created life form to pass those experiences on to it.
Therefore, God pushes all life to survive if it can - hence the fight/flight concept. Fight for life or run to survive.
So, we might add fight/flight to the list of personality aspects.

You will have noticed, of course, that these first three aspects of personality in animals;
1. Ego
2. Fear
3. Fight/flight
are closely connected. So close as to be almost one aspect.

If an animal did not have ego (desire to survive), fear of attack or starvation, and also the fight/flight aspect, it would not survive for long in the wild.

Brotherly love between most individual animals is rare indeed.

It is usually only humans who can take disparate animals under their wing, so to speak, and teach them to lose that fear and that desire to kill.

We have all seen the way a human can adopt widely different species of animals, whilst young, and encourage them to live together in peace and harmony.

That is also an aspect of the God force, this time love, overpowering the natural desire of animals to have fear, and to live in harmony, knowing that its human friend will care for its every need, and so the animals lay aside their basic instincts of hunting, or of being hunted and live as God first, or perhaps we should say last, as intended.

Animals live as they do for the moment, because the way life is constructed, the pendulum swing from dark to light, has for a long time been in the dark, evil, we could almost say, part of existence.

However, we are now moving into a long period of light and the day will come when man not only stops fighting himself but will start to care for the animal kingdom and carnivorous animals will be fed with synthetic meat, since they no longer have to hunt to survive.

Gradually, these animals will lose the fear and fight/flight aspects so prevalent now and will live in peace with all animals.

It will be man who will bring this about on a global scale, rather like he can do it on a small scale in his home environment, when he adopts animals and teaches them to live together in harmony and brotherly love.

But for the moment, apart from the so-called domestic creatures that man has adopted for many millennia - cats and dogs, etc., - the vast majority of animals live apart from mankind and, generally, live in fear of man, as they do with most other creatures. They either fear being caught as prey or spend much of their time hunting.

But, to go back to the personality aspects of animals, we mentioned ego - the desire to survive, fear of either starving or of being eaten as prey and we should, of course, mention the desire to mate - sex drive.

With many animals this has developed into a pattern that enables the young to be born at the most favourable time to enable the young to survive.

For instance, with birds, regardless of whether they are carnivorous or seed eating, they generally mate in late winter, and/or early spring, so that by the time the eggs hatch, food in the form of seeds or flies is available for the young.

In the case of mammals, it is a similar story, except that the young have a greater chance of surviving in warm weather rather than in the depths of winter so, logic and necessity has encouraged most wild animals to mate at a time most favourable to the survival of the young.

This process is interesting in that, like plants, most animals are instinctively aware of the seasons.

As you can imagine, animals do not consciously observe the different seasons, being almost always in the present moment and, unlike humans, do not concern themselves with the idea of mating until the appropriate moment arrives.
Then, with many species, changes occur.
With some birds, for example, brighter plumage appears, they may start to construct nests or look for holes in which to lay eggs and, generally, prepare for the mating season.
With mammals, other aspects of behaviour occur. The males tend to become more aggressive, and the females start to produce pheromones that will stimulate the sex drive in males, whilst the production of hormones will prepare the females to become pregnant.

We might question what process stimulates this change of attitude.
It is sometimes referred to as a biological clock gently ticking the year away until the mating season arrives.
In fact, what is happening is an aspect of personality is pre-programmed by the God spirit to awaken this dormant shift according to the best time for mating of each species.

We should expand on this further.
Everything is vibration, and as time, in as far as it exists, is also vibration, it is possible for a year to be divided by the number of Hertz (cycles per second) that planet Earth vibrates to and thus a chosen moment can trigger the mating cycle.

Let us repeat this to make it quite clear, although it is not difficult to understand.
Everything vibrates and, in effect, everything is vibration. Although each animal has its own unique vibration, with regard to the mating season effect, the individual vibration of each animal plays only a small part.
Planet Earth vibrates. Due to the huge size of Earth compared to any animal, the vibrations being emitted by the planet override any vibrations of any animal or group of animals.

The planet Earth rotates around the sun in one year - if we ignore the slight discrepancies as measured by man - so the exact number of vibrations in the year is known. They are used by life in a number of ways but, in this case, what we call nature, which is collective wisdom in the animal kingdom, decides for each animal or group of animals, how many cycles of vibrations should pass before the mating season is activated.

Equally, the number of cycles of planet Earth's vibrations are known before that cycle fades and either the female creature is pregnant or she isn't.
It is all quite simply a personality aspect of an animal being aware of the number of cycles of Earth's frequency that need to pass in order to trigger the mating cycle.

We will add that what we have described, although true, is not completely true.
What really happens is that, if we can imagine planet Earth to be rather like a giant programmable alarm clock, just like an alarm clock, when it is programmed to ring at a

certain time, a flag is attached to the timing mechanism and when the flag is triggered the alarm rings.

The different cycles of the Earth are rather like that.

As the planet vibrates so, from time to time, flags are triggered which tell certain events to appear.

One of these important ones is what we call the mating season. We should, perhaps, mention that this flag does not activate as a solitary alarm. There are, in fact, a number of these flags that activate around the world according to how the seasons arrive and according to the different species.

Obviously, spring arrives in a country like Australia at a different time than it does in the Northern Hemisphere so a mating season alert will be activated at a much different time in the South than it does in the North.

But everything is well organised so that life unfolds as it should.

The subject of these different alarm systems, flags, is an interesting study in its own right and would merit a long dissertation to explain but is not really the subject of this book, so we will not go further into it for the moment and continue with our investigation of the personality traits of animals.

So, we have got to the knowledge of;
* Being alive,
* Fear,
* Fight/flight,
* And, sex drive, which we just mentioned.

Then of course, we arrive at the moment when the young are born.

Now, we will say that some animals, particularly those that lay eggs - snakes, turtles and some similar animals - just lay their eggs somewhere and abandon their offspring to their fate, but the vast amount of creatures devote the greatest attention to their offspring and even the most devoted human could not do more for them.

We tend to call this "motherly love", but we must also say that, with many species, the fathers take their fair share in caring for the young also.

We are familiar with the term "motherly love" but "fatherly love" does not have the same ring to it, so we will continue to call it "motherly love".

So, we can add that to our list.

Now, we are also aware that, mixed with motherly love is the willingness to fight, to the death if necessary, to protect the young.

This is a part of motherly love but is also an almost separate aspect, in that it flies completely in the face of the fight/flight aspect of normal behaviour.

So, although it only occurs when the parents have young to protect, nevertheless, let us add it to the list of personality traits.

The next one we will examine is what we might call "family unity".

There are some animals that live solitary lives, only coming together at mating season, but most animals join in groups. Sometimes small family units, sometimes in huge numbers.

We are all familiar with the huge shoals of fish that used to fill the oceans and the huge herds of American Bison that roamed the American prairies, until decimated by man.

But even now, if left in peace, the majority of animals will live together peacefully and will grow in numbers, if not hunted by man, until they can reach extraordinary proportions.

Of course, in certain circumstances, with locusts, cockroaches, fleas and so on, it is better that they be kept under control, but it must have been a wonderful sight in America before the white settlers arrived, to see a herd of buffalo passing, so large that it took all day for them to pass.

Perhaps, the day that man loses his destructive instinct, these herds will return. Planet Earth is huge and there is room for all beings, both man and beast.

So, we can add this herd instinct to the list of personality aspects of most animals.

Our list of personality features is growing.

There is one feature that is quite rare but is of importance because, although it is not very common in animals at the moment, it is an aspect that we expect to grow in the future as Ascension progresses. And it is this… love.

True love between adult animals is quite rare at the moment but there are, nevertheless, a surprising number of animals that create pairs and these pairs remain together until one of them demises.

This is love and it is delightful to observe such a pair encounter each other when quite young and grow to old age sharing their lives, mating each season and always remaining faithful to each other, caring for each other's needs and delighting in being in each other's company.

This is true love, probably more intense than the love that any two humans might have. Usually, with humans, there is the suspicion that one of the couple might be unfaithful one day, so human love is often tinged with fear, fear of being betrayed. With animals that mate for life, no such fear exists. The two animals bond for life and there is never any thought of one betraying the other. It is true, unconditional partnership. True love.

So, although it is not a general feature amongst all animals yet, we hope that it will become so, and it is certainly an aspect of personality available, if yet dormant in most animals, so we will add that to the list. Love.

So, let us turn to another aspect of animal personality and that is the desire to live solitary existences.

We mentioned that many animals live in groups and it is easy to find large numbers of animals that do live in groups.

It is always dangerous to generalise, because there are always exceptions but, quite often these animals that live in groups, packs, herds, are vegetarian. Thus, can thousands of a particular species live together and still find sufficient to eat because they eat grasses, bushes and various other plants.

Naturally, we do find some carnivorous species that live in groups; lions, wolves, etc., but these groups are fairly small. It would not be possible to have carnivorous species grouping in huge numbers, as they would not be able to feed huge numbers, so the carnivorous ones tend to live in extended family groups.

But, within each group, whether herbivore or carnivore, there is always the desire to be the dominant entity.
With some of these groups, the dominant male does his best to be the only one mating with the females, and there is at least the wolf breed that has a dominant male and female, and they are the only ones who produce offspring.
The reason for this is obvious.
If weak animals reproduced, weak genes would be passed on to the young and the race would grow feeble, but if only the strongest breed, strongest genes are passed on, thus making the species better able to survive.
So, we have another aspect of personality that we might call "genetic superiority".

We hope you can see that we are not using these personality traits with any attempt at giving them pseudo-scientific names. We tried to give as clear a picture as we can as to the effects of these traits, so that no one has to struggle to comprehend.
Once again, we could go on endlessly finding personality aspects of animals, but we will stop here and just résumé the main aspects:
* Ego
* Fear
* Fight/flight
* Sex drive
* Mating season
* Motherly love
* Family unity
* Herd instinct
* Love
* Genetic superiority

CHAPTER SIX

AN INTRODUCTION TO ALIENS - PART 1

Logic would dictate, that next we discuss humanity but we have covered the subject of humanity in great detail in other books and essays, so we feel that we do not need to repeat what we have already described as fully as we could.

Therefore, as you may remember from the Foreword we said that this book would be devoted to what you call aliens, so we will jump to discussing this topic.

You may have questioned why we have spent so much of this book to a discussion of the personality traits of other objects, but the reason was to give you as clear a picture as possible of the aspects of personalities that all things have, so we hope that you will not think that the previous chapters were a waste of time.
We want you to understand that all things have personality aspects and the more sentient a thing is, the more personality traits it has.

So, assuming that what we referred to as aliens do exist, and, assuming that they are much more advanced compared to anything on Earth, humans included, one would expect them to have a large number of personality traits. We will examine these traits later as, first, we need to discuss whether or not whatever are referred to as aliens really do exist, where their home is and all that we can possibly describe about them.

If we try to examine alien life from just looking at evidence found on Earth we come up with a somewhat mixed bag to say the least.

The first thing we notice is that, if we look back into the past, we can find little or no hard evidence that we have been visited by alien races.

Let us, for the moment, ignore recent times, with reports of down craft, captured crew members and the countless photographs and films presented to us and just consider what still exists from long ago.
After all, if aliens were visiting planet Earth from long ago, one might expect to find some hard evidence.

But first of all, let us try to decide on what to call these beings, assuming they exist. Sometimes they are referred to as extra-terrestrials (ET's).
Extra is a Latin word implying 'outside of', 'not part of' and terrestrial obviously implies planet Earth.
Therefore, the word extraterrestrial implies beings that come from somewhere outside of Earth.
Now, the implication of this is that we are considering physical beings who live on some planet remote from Earth.

If it can be believed, what we have stated, that there is no physical life on any planet other than Earth, then the word Extra-Terrestrial would have no meaning. So, let us ignore that misnomer.

Then they are referred to as 'aliens'.

Alien implies not known to a particular culture. Also, the word alien can have somewhat negative connotations; alien food sometimes being unpleasant to people unfamiliar with the taste.

This sounds a bit more promising as aliens tend to be unknown to the majority of people and are certainly distasteful to most.

But the question has not been answered as to where they come from and to call someone alien, as in 'illegal alien', implies knowledge of their place of origin.

We can only call someone alien if we are sure that they do not come from planet Earth. But we have no certitude at this point as to where they come from.

Let us give a little, childish example, to demonstrate the point. Many people are convinced that fairy folk; gnomes, elves, pixies, etc., exist. Assuming they do, we do not refer to them as aliens, as we presume that they originate on and from Earth. We have no proof of this but we accept that they exist, are interdimensional but are linked to planet Earth, so we don't call them aliens.

And yet these beings, the visitors, we call aliens, despite not knowing where they come from.

However, we must call them something if we wish to discuss them, so we will refer to them as aliens although, as this book unfolds, it is probable that we will find the word inappropriate.

Therefore, until and unless we can find a more appropriate appellation, we will call them aliens.

So, to return to the past. If it is true that aliens have flying machines that are sometimes referred to as 'unidentified flying objects' (UFOs) or flying saucers and if it is true that they crash onto the surface of planet Earth today, it would be fair to assume that they would have crashed in the past and yet it is rare that we come across any.

There is some evidence that an aircraft called a Vimana has been discovered in a cave but, apart from rumour, has anyone actually seen it?

The only evidence that is presented to us are rock paintings depicting UFOs and creatures in strange dress, plus some stones carved into the shapes of flying craft and/or alien looking beings.

It is also fair to say that any evidence discovered today depicting alien visits is immediately secreted away from public gaze.

So, the truth is that we have virtually no proof from the past that aliens, or their modes of transport, ever existed.

Now we come to modern times. Things are much different today but real proof is just as elusive.

One could say that the modern era of ufology started in 1947 with the Roswell incident(s), although there were downed craft before that time.

But public awareness really started in July 1947 with the somewhat bungled Roswell incident and its cover up.

The actual details of this event - of which there was more than one - is not the subject of this book, so we will not go into the details of it.

The record is, of course, available in the Akashic Records for those willing to learn to enter that place, so we will not give any details here.

So, we do seem to have some proof that beings from elsewhere do exist and have created a variety of craft.

The problems as far as the public are concerned, are many and varied.

To those few who have genuinely seen a UFO, or have interacted with alien beings, there is no doubt that these entities exist. But the percentage of people who have had a genuine experience, in terms of the world's population, is infinitesimal.

From our investigations of those who claim to be experiencers, the vast majority are creating with their imaginations these events, they were not real.

Of the few who have had experiences, quite often mind wiping technology is used to eradicate any memories so, as we said, those who have had experiences and can remember them, the number is very small indeed.

Then, of course, the various governmental, military and quasi military groups charged with hiding this truth about aliens, is very effective at covering up any sightings, downed craft and captured entities.

It seems to be most government's number one priority to pretend that we are not visited by beings from 'elsewhere', wherever that 'elsewhere' might be.

Lastly, it is interesting to note the number of people who are unwilling to face facts regarding visitations and are only too willing to accept the stories put out that sightings are mistaken identity.

Perhaps we could spend a moment looking at why authorities spend such a vast amount of time, effort and financial resources to cover up these visitations.

After all, if planet Earth is being visited by groups from elsewhere, one would have thought it of paramount importance to inform the public.

But the opposite obtains.

It is interesting to note that, immediately following the bungled Roswell incident, where it was admitted that a UFO had crashed - then hotly denied - committees and groups were set up at many levels to control and deny the truth concerning UFO visitations.

It is the speed that all this was set up that raises questions.

Usually, if anything similar occurs - immigration by huge numbers of young people from deprived countries for example - a large amount of time passes in studying the problem before coming to a conclusion, if a conclusion is reached, but in the case of 'alien immigrants', action was taken virtually overnight on a worldwide basis that clamped a lid on any revelations.

One wonders just how such a speedy action was achieved, especially when one considers the so-called Cold War that was in full swing, in which groups of countries opposed other groups of countries and yet, as soon as demonstrative proof was released to the public, every country in the world instantly agreed to deny the evidence.

Could it be that some other force than politicians were behind the cover up and, if so, what was and is that group and what was the motive?

Our main interest is the alien visitors and not the beings who control governments, so we will investigate that subject later.

For the moment, let us consider why it was so important to hide the truth, sufficiently important, that many people were assassinated to keep the secret intact - as it is at the moment of writing this book.

A number of reasons have been put forward to justify denial, some of whom seemed reasonable at the time but really do not hold water today.

The first considered was general panic among the world's population, if it was suddenly announced that planet Earth was being visited by beings of vastly superior intelligence and technology than humans had at that time. This was no doubt true at the time, 1947, because planet Earth had recently been rocked by two terrible wars and the history of Earth had, for millennia, been one of constant wars by invading forces.

Thus, it was assumed that any visitors would have evil intentions and so it was deemed wise to hide any and all such visitations until arms of equal power to the so-called invaders could be manufactured.

Next, there was fear that religions would be found out to be based on incorrect information. This is understandable, as most religions have created stories to explain the various events recorded in religious texts. Although to anyone awake, it is obvious that some of the stories in religious books could well have alien intervention behind them, the stories have always been twisted to imply angelic intervention, despite there being no firm knowledge that angels exist.

But time has given a veneer of respectability to the concept of angels, whereas aliens would be new and thus seen as a menace.

In more recent times, people have started to query the propulsion systems, both silent and capable of extraordinary aerobatics feats including, of course, anti-gravity.

At the time, Earth technology was very primitive and relied on the use of fossil fuels - just as it does today - where as it was obvious that UFOs did not use fossil fuels at all.

So, economic considerations were discussed and, if the technology used by aliens was released to the public, it would ring the death knell to all the vast profits companies make from fossil fuels.

But, the most important consideration was one that was never discussed publicly. Planet Earth had, for many hundreds of thousands of years, been under the control of a group of etheric beings called Archons.

We have discussed this group in other books and talks.

They have controlled all governments and most religions for a long time and are, actually, humanity's greatest enemy.

Now, the Archons are very familiar with alien groups of all types.

We will discuss the personalities of aliens later but we will say that, like all people, some are good, some are evil and some are neutral.

Now, as soon as the Archons learnt of the Roswell incident, they swung into action and informed all the world leaders to deny and cover up any alien intervention.

The reason is this.

The good aliens are very much aware of Archons and what harm they have caused to planet Earth and the Archons were terrified that the good aliens would reveal the presence of Archons to us and explain the harm they have caused and even suggest ways and means of getting rid of them.

At that time - 1947 - the general public were sublimely ignorant of the presence in the etheric realms of these Archons that were and are overshadowing many politicians and world leaders.

The Archons wanted to keep it that way.

You may have heard of an American president that had a meeting with an alien group. These were good people and offered to guide the world towards peace. Their offer was refused by the human's present, who were already under the control of the Archons.

In the meantime, the Archons contacted a group of evil aliens who, soon after the first meeting with the good aliens, had a meeting with the same president and his cohorts, who immediately agreed to work with the evil ones.

Once again, these politicians and church leaders who met with both groups, had no option but to refuse the first group of aliens and agree to the second - the evil ones - because all concerned were under the psychic control of the Archons.

Thus, a treaty was agreed to between the people of planet Earth and this evil group of aliens, that you know as Grey's.

Both parties were and are influenced by the Archons.

As we have previously said, the time of the Archons is drawing to a close and they will, eventually, be chased from influencing your leaders.

People have often asked why disclosure has not taken place but, from what we have stated above, you can see that disclosure will never happen while the Archons are controlling your leaders.

If the good aliens were revealed publicly, they would mention the Archons and the harm they have caused.

It is the fact that most people have never heard of Archons that enables them to operate in secret.

If their presence were revealed to the public, steps would be taken to remove their minions from power.

So, do not expect disclosure to come from any governmental agencies.

You may have noticed that we mentioned a link between the Archons and aliens.

Archons live primarily in the etheric realms which, like all areas, there are more than one of.

At the lowest end, the etheric realms, touch 3D reality (the one in which you live) while, at the opposite end they touch the astral planes.

The Archons have the ability to move up and down the etheric realms and it is at the higher end that they come into contact with aliens, because aliens live in the astral realms, or rather in the many sub-frequencies of the astral realms.

Now, you may have wondered why we started this book off with several chapters about the personality of stones, plants and animals, when we said that this book would be about aliens?

The reason is that there is a link between all life, and we tried, by describing the personality aspects of various life forms that inhabit the planet Earth, to demonstrate that there were definitely links between all things. We did not discuss humanity, because we have already done so but we would like you, if we may suggest, to think of humanity's personality aspects when you consider what we said about the personality trends of all life. You should be able to notice that we said that stones, etc., although apparently lifeless, have nevertheless a number of personality aspects. Plants have the same, plus a few more, animals, once again, have the same basic aspects but, being more sentient than either stones or plants, have an enlarged range of personality traits at its disposal.

If we were to describe the personality traits of humans you would notice all the ones that applied to other life but with extra ones added.

Thus, there is a clear growth of personalities from stones to plants to animals and then to humans.

This is logical, as all is one, but there are degrees of awareness to this oneness.

Further, all these personality traits are contained within the multitude of sub-dimensions of the 8 main dimensions.

We wish you to understand that it has never been clear where aliens come from.

The reasons are several.

The Grey's were instructed by the Archons never to reveal that they come from interdimensional areas, because it might have been possible for people to forge a link between them and the Archons. The Archon's secret to success has always been that people do not know that they exist and so, if a Grey alien blurted out that they were in touch with the Archon's, the game would be up.

So, the Grey's were instructed to say anything but the truth. Thus, the story about Zeta Reticuli was concocted, but it is not true.

In the case of good aliens, until the publication of this book, very little was known about inter-dimensions.

Indeed, although this information was known a long time ago and mentioned in some Indian texts, due to translations by people who did not understand about the dimensions, the translations were often less than perfect.

Added to this is the unfortunate fact that many, indeed most, of the people who claim to have been in contact with aliens were inventing it and had no idea where they really came from, so they invented stories based on old wives' tales and said that they came from various star clusters; Pleiades, Sirius, etc. This also is nonsense and yet a whole myth has been created around it.

People claim to have met beautiful aliens from the Pleiades, have been taken aboard UFOs and flown around the galaxy or that they are hybrids, usually, with Pleiadian blood

- everyone wants to be special and no one wants to come from a bad alien group - so everyone and his dog, as the saying goes, claims to be a Pleiadian hybrid.

It is staggering to see the number of people who write books and give lectures on their experiences, entirely fictitious, about their interactions with aliens.

Now, we will explain clearly and, we hope, once and for all just where these aliens come from and who they really are but we must first clear the board of all the nonsense that has built up since 1947.

We will say this about a group who are often associated with aliens and that is a group of people periodically known as the Tall Whites or the Nordics. They are the same group of people. They have recently started to reveal themselves on Earth and seem to have a mixed personality. Some people claim that they are a noble group and some say that they are wicked, having worked with the Reptilians and people like Adolf Hitler.

No doubt, like most people, some are good and some are less than good but one thing we can say, and be sure of, is they want to preserve the planet Earth, because they are from Earth.

Their origin is not for us to disclose, but we give away no secrets that they come from hollowed-out areas below the surface of planet Earth.

For reasons best known to themselves, they decided to move underground a long time ago and, having avoided the extermination level events that have rocked planet Earth from time to time, and not having fallen under the control of the Archons, have been able to develop many advanced technologies and systems of government, that have greatly benefited them.

They are extremely concerned by the destructive attitudes of some military factions and are very much against the use of atomic weapons, which could, and is, causing irreparable harm to Earth.

Those of you who are old enough to remember the countless underground nuclear tests that were carried out will not know, but those tests were carried out by those under the control of the Archons, who hoped to damage the underground facilities of these Tall Whites - who are, themselves, enemies of the Archons.

Fortunately, no harm was caused to the Tall Whites, who tolerated these nuclear explosions for a while before taking steps to put a stop to them.

But, we repeat, they are from planet Earth herself, although when questioned as to their origins, usually site the Pleiades to put people off their scent. They do not want us humans delving into their underground domains.

There is at least one other group who also live underground but it is their wish to remain secret at this time, so we will not betray their secret.

CHAPTER SEVEN

AN INTRODUCTION TO ALIENS - PART 2

In this chapter, we are going to attempt to explain the origins of what are known as aliens.

Now, we warn you that the subject is somewhat complicated and cannot be explained in just a few lines.

We spent time in explaining the different personality aspects of Earth creatures and you will have noticed that none of what we mentioned could be described as physical, although the effects of these personality traits are very often seen in physicality.

In another work, we have described the human body - just to talk about humans - as having two aspects, the physical body and the non-physical aspect.

Further, we have spent a great deal of time, effort and ink, to describe as fully as we good, the vast range of non-physical aspects there is to all life, some more noticeable, as in the case of a human, than in the case of a stone.

But, as we constantly remind you, all is one and so a stone and a human have the same potential, even though, in the case of a stone, much of it seems dormant.

Lastly, in this book, we have described the various and many sub-dimensions to all the eight main dimensions, and we placed a lot of emphasis on the personality traits as they apply to various aspects of life.

Those of you who are familiar with our writings, know that we tend to try to explain things as carefully and as simply as we can and so, sometimes, we seem to ramble from apparent subject to subject but we hope that, by now, you realise we have taken great care to explain in simple language, all the various subfactors required to comprehend what can be difficult subjects.

So, all that we just mentioned above applies not only to all that exists in physicality, but also applies in the non-physical universe as well.

People have the impression that the non-physical world is somehow different from the physical world and, to a certain extent it is, but the main aspects of life remain exactly the same despite whether one is considering physicality or the non-physical worlds.

May we say before we proceed, that we have made a change to a word that we frequently use.

Up till now, we spoke of physical and spiritual worlds.

Physical obviously meant the world and entities you see around you, but we had a problem with the word spiritual.

There are actually two meanings to the word spiritual.

The first means something that is not physical - spirit, soul, auras, heaven, hell and all the other things we speak about, and the second meaning implies holy.

Now, as you know, things can be non-physical but far from holy.

So, to avoid confusion, we have decided that, from now on, we will use the words non-physical to describe something that is invisible, part of the auric dimensions, and the word spiritual to describe something or someone that is holy. This will help us in our descriptions of things and, we hope, will avoid confusion on your part when deciding if we are talking about something outside of the physical realms as opposed to holy.

We mentioned this at this point because, in dealing with aliens we are almost always in the non-physical aspect of life.

It may also help if we clear the ground regarding the various physical 'aliens' that are seen.

As we previously stated, the vast majority of sightings reported are fake.

Now, some of these are just mistaken identity by a person who sees a strange looking person or flying craft, some of them are deliberate fraud by those who have nothing better to do and create sightings of people or craft in a computer, and some are deliberate false trails put out by various government agencies who want to muddy the waters.

True aliens are non-physical, as we will explain so, obviously, no sightings can be of aliens.

However, it will be helpful if we can describe and discount the beings that are seen and the body's collected following downed UFOs.

Most popular are what are known as 'the Grey's'.

These are creatures, some about 4 ft tall and some slightly larger, with the well known bulbous heads, large lenticular eyes and almost no facial features, apart from their eyes. They are all robots, programmed life forms (PLF), although they are so frequently seen in relation to UFOs, that some people claim them to be a race - usually from the future - that have returned to our time to collect DNA to correct some genetic fault created through inbreeding or some similar unfortunate turn of events.

This seems to be a story accepted even by the military, who have to deal with them, that is just a ridiculous story created, either by the Grey robots, or their masters or by the military to explain their presence on Earth.

If the people who believed the story had the slightest notion of how life is recorded in the Akashic Record, they would realise that each frame of life is protected, exactly to stop any modification to be made to life.

Each and every event is lived for a fraction of a second, is recorded in the Akashic Record and the next frame, the next microsecond, is lived, only to be stored and thus life goes on.

So, if some event occurred that was displeasing to a future generation, they might well return from that future, to some moment in the past and observe events occurring at this previous time, but in no way could they change the events.

They occur just once, are recorded for all time, but cannot be altered.

The classic puzzle in relation to this is the 'grandfather story'. It goes like this.

If a person returns from the future to a moment in the past and kills his grandfather, that person could not be born, needing his grandparents to create, eventually … him!

This childish story has been used to claim that time travel is not possible but, of course, time travel is possible but the life of the grandfather, once all the countless frames of time/space are over, and the events recorded, is protected for that very reason.

Could you imagine, for example, the confusion that would be caused by, say, one side winning a war and then someone going back in time to change the past so that the other side won and then, shortly after, someone going back in time to reverse the decision again and each side going on endlessly like that? It would be preposterous, because you can be sure that if it were possible to change the past, it would constantly be done to virtually all things in all domains.

It may be a good subject for a comic film but, in reality, would cause chaos.

So, the Archangels responsible for controlling life, quite simply created a way of not being able to change the past.

One would imagine that aliens from the future would have sufficient knowledge to know that the past cannot be interfered with, so they are either counting on the military with whom they are in contact not having the knowledge or intelligence to know that the Grey's are lying, or there is some flaw in the story.

We have, of course, discussed this in the video that was made but it is worth repeating, so that all who read this book are clear that the past cannot be changed.

While we are discussing these little Grey robots, we might as well mention that those who have been autopsied, following the demise in a UFO crash, or following their imprisonment, the doctors performing the autopsies have been astonished to note a certain amount of vegetable matter within them.

This gives a clue as to the extreme age of the original plans for constructing these robots. We have mentioned that long years ago, the Archangels experimented with producing creatures from plant material, long before flesh and blood creatures were thought of, so it is highly possible that these robots were first created at that time and then modified somewhat when flesh and blood beings were introduced onto Earth.

If this is true it gives some idea of how long aliens have been interested in Earth.

It is also interesting to note that the original programmed life forms have remained unmodified all that time. We will discuss the reasons for this later.

To end our brief discussion on programmed life forms (Grey robots), we will say that their IQ is about 80, just sufficient to carry out the commands of their masters, who direct operations by telepathy, following the antics of these robots by using their eyes as cameras.

People who have interacted with these robots have noticed that they do, indeed, seem to be soulless, heartless entities, incapable of speech and incapable of any emotion.

The reason is, of course, that they are just robots - machines directed to perform certain acts but not capable of independent thought.

Next, people report seeing creatures resembling, somewhat, Praying Mantis.
Once again, the majority of these reports are fictitious, but they do exist. Their form was chosen because they are actually quite human in their ability to move - standing on their hind legs, having active forearms, eyes and other features not dissimilar to humans.
So, although these also are robots, PLFs, it was clever of some alien race to note that they could be constructed and instructed to perform acts not dissimilar to that of a human.
Generally, the IQ is slightly higher than that of a Grey, but they also just obey orders given telepathically by their masters, who remain in the etheric or astral realms.

Recently, there have been reports about a variety of creatures who have physical bodies and who are supposed to be aliens.
There have been reports of meetings, of councils who come together to discuss how the future of planet Earth will unfold, but we regret to say that there is no truth in any of this.

It must be clearly understood that aliens are not physical, and if they could be seen at all, would just be balls of energy although, in fact, the type of energy they are created from would exclude even an energy ball forming. We will discuss the aliens in detail a bit later. At the moment we are considering more what they are not, than what they are.
We remember that we stated at the beginning of this chapter, that we said we would discuss the origins of aliens, but we hope you will forgive us if we get out of the way some of the robots that are often assumed to be aliens.
So, we suggest that you listen with the greatest caution to people giving lectures claiming to be Ambassadors for alien races, communicating with them regularly and attending meetings and so on.
We are not accusing these people of fraud. The reasons that they make the statements they do might be completely innocent but we can assure you that none of it actually happens.

Obviously, there might be some people who are creating the stories in order to build a career for themselves. After all, if someone makes outlandish claims, who can say that he is fabricating the story? No one at the moment knows the truth about aliens - which is why we are releasing this book to you - so anyone can claim anything, and who can deny it? We hope that if you will believe what we are going to tell you in this book, you will have a firm foundation of facts concerning this mysterious group - the aliens.

It is also a strange fact that the more bizarre the story people come up with, the more people seem ready to believe it.
It is also true that if one creates a false story and one repeats it often enough, it comes to be accepted as true. However, as far as we are concerned, we do not wish anyone to remain in the dark of any subject and, as we know the true story about aliens, we are happy to tell you, and if it upsets those perpetuating falsehoods, so be it.

But, we will say that there are a number of reasons that people think they are interacting with aliens, when they are not.
Some people might have mental illnesses and, having followed a subject found on internet, for example, think that it is happening to them.

Then there are people who have worked for the military and have a variety of false messages implanted in their minds, and who are convinced that they are, or have been, in contact with aliens.

There are military groups who deliberately create and implant false memories so that, in the end, the public do not know what or who to believe and so dismiss the whole affair.

So, there are a number of perfectly reasonable reasons why people make these false claims about aliens.

As we said, if something is repeated often enough it is accepted as true, hence we have countless people who claim to be channeling aliens, have met aliens, have flown with aliens or have alien blood.

Virtually all of this is not true.

So, what can we say about aliens and where they reside?

This is where the story gets complicated, because aliens really do not live anywhere.

As we said, they are invisible to humans, and it is only their created life forms - robots - that interact with us.

The true aliens never, or almost never, come into your 3D domain. They cannot. They do not have the capacity, with very few exceptions, of entering 3D reality.

The reason, strange as this is going to sound, is that they are products of personalities.

Obviously, this needs a great deal of explanation and we do not expect all of you to be able to accept what we are going to say.

Collective wisdom has long imagined that alien visitors are flesh and blood 'people', not dissimilar to Earth humans, except that they come from some planet somewhere in the galaxy; the moon, Mars, the Pleiades, the Sirius star system, Zeta Reticuli and so on, and the robots, when questioned, have confirmed this.

The reason why aliens would say such a thing is understandable, as the truth as to their home areas would have been dismissed as lies, where as a lie concerning the origin sounds believable.

After all, if people live on the surface of planet Earth, it makes sense that aliens would be physical entities living on the surface of some other planet somewhere in the galaxy, that would resemble somewhat Earth with regards to its geography, water, oxygen, etc.

Scientists and astronomers even now, if they are not denying the existence of aliens, are scanning the galaxy and proudly announcing to a believing world the discovery of planets, just at the right distance from a sun, containing just the right mixture of elements to support life.

It may be that, one day, humans, when they develop space travel, will visit some of these planets and will be able to wander about without using spacesuits, but they will visit these planets and find them bereft of any form of sentient life. None of them contain aliens, animals, fish or insects.

The only planet with life on it is this one.

Now, we must leave the aliens for a moment to remind you that planet Earth, indeed the whole galaxy, does not exist.

It is an imaginary world created by the Archangels and maintained by collective consciousness.

Further, you do not exist in the physical form you see in a mirror. No one exists as a solid physical being.
You, and us, are all just auras, non-physical and we have all been programmed by the Archangels to imagine that we are real, flesh and blood beings, living on a solid planet, in the physical universe.

As we have said, the illusion is so strong, that it seems real, but the truth is that it is all just astral matter brought together by individual and collective consciousness - imagination - to create this giant theatrical piece that we call reality.

So, this being so, whether you can accept it or not, it follows that aliens could not be solid, flesh and blood beings, living on solid planets.
Even if they had been programmed like us to believe that all this is real, the truth is that they must be, like us, astral forms living an illusionary existence and just imagining themselves to be real.

But they have not been programmed to believe that they are physical as you will see in a moment.
Only those humans or animals destined to come to Earth are programmed like this.
The Archangels never waste energy and, as what we referred to as aliens, were never destined to interact with planet Earth, the programing stopped with all that was destined to enter so-called physicality.

The truth concerning life, is that we are all non-existent nothingness, living nowhere. We do not exist, being only a thought in God's imagination.
We have briefly said this before, but have not pushed the idea on to you, because it seems so impossible.

We would be the first to agree that life seems so real, planet Earth and the galaxy seems so real but, as we have tried to explain, using an onion as an example, if we peel off the layers of skin, we arrive at nothing.
The onion ceases to exist. It only existed when it was whole and there is no life force to be found at its centre. Its life, when it was whole, was just an illusion.

Now, although we did introduce the concept that nothing actually exists, we did not explore the idea, because we just wanted you to get used to the concept that nothing exists.
We are sure that even now most of you will not be able to accept that you do not actually exist in the form that you see, that you have been programmed to see.
But, it is the moment to try to expand your mind, to accept that you do not exist in the way that seems so real.
We want you to accept the possibility that planet Earth and the galaxy, air, water, land, space - none of this exists.

All that exists is nothing!

All that you think exists is illusion.

The only thing that exists is this creative force we call God, and God is a non-existent force - as far as we can tell - but that has infinite creative power.

So, God told his Archangels to create this vast illusion. We have already hinted that all the books we have given you, all the essays, all the videos that you may have watched that explained life in such detail, was and is explaining illusion, but this illusion seems so real that we accept as real and can spend a lot of time and energy to explain in the most minute detail, this incredibly complicated and complex multi-layered existence, that so much effort has gone into making and maintaining.

And yet, the truth is that it is not real.

Now, why are we explaining all this?

Quite simply because, if life as we see it is not real, then aliens cannot be real.

If nothing actually exists, then aliens cannot exist.

But, if we can see the robots that come here, if we can see the UFOs that come here; see them, film them, back engineer the crashed or captured ones, there must be something going on.

They obviously seem real to us.

But, you will notice that we mentioned the programmed life forms (the robots), we mentioned the UFOs, but we never mentioned the aliens themselves!

Why did we not?

This will be the subject of the next chapter.

CHAPTER 8

THE MYSTERY REVEALED

In the last chapter, we discussed at great length, that nothing really exists in the physical manner that you can see, and that we have explained in great depth - perhaps more clearly than life has ever been explained - in previous works.

Now, we are going to have to join two disparate elements together if we want to make sense of the lives we all lead, and that alien life is part of.

The basic truth about life is that nothing exists. We have explained this as carefully and as fully as we can, but it is such a ridiculously bizarre concept that we do understand that many, indeed, most of you will totally reject the very idea.

Even the most open minded of you will have the greatest difficulty in accepting that you do not exist, because you obviously do or you would not be reading this book.

We, who dictate this book would not exist.

The person who writes our thoughts down would not exist.

None of the electronic systems employed to create the book would exist.

The paper, the printers, the printing machines would not exist.

In short, if nothing existed this book could not exist and you who are reading it do not exist - but clearly, all that we mentioned above does exist. The result is that you are reading that we are saying that nothing exists!

So, how can we resolve this conundrum, and what has it to do with aliens - who clearly exist also?

So, we will repeat what we have already said many times. Nothing exists but this force we call God.

This force has many names and it is unfortunate that the word, the name 'God' has been adopted by various religions and given a holy, remote context, that makes it quite impossible to discuss God in any rational manner to most religious people because, as soon as we do, we are treading on their toes, encroaching on their sacred territory, and explosions occur verbally. Thus, often, it is quite impossible to discuss God.

We would be the first to admit that we do not know what God is because, as he (it) doesn't exist in any manner, shape or form, how can anyone possibly describe or investigate nothing.

However, as nothing does not imply that it ultimately applies to all, we have to scratch our heads and admit that there must be degrees of nothing, or you and us would not exist.

So, are we hedging our bets with regard to saying that nothing exists?

One could answer that perhaps we are, but we will soldier on because to discuss the alien subject we need to have an absolutely clear picture in our minds between the concept of nothingness, and the world in which we all seem to live.

To understand alien life, if we do not understand the difference between nothingness and apparent reality, we cannot understand alien life, where it comes from, how it exists, and what the agendas are.

So, we hope you will excuse us if we continue to try and establish the link between nothingness, and the life we see and experience.

We do not have all the answers to all the questions concerning life and nothingness but, thanks to our human Archangelic friends, who have been so kind as to share their knowledge and wisdom with us, we do know some things, sufficient to be able to share what we know with you. If we did not think it was true, if we were not sure of our facts, we would say nothing. So, we present to you what we are sure of and leave it up to you to accept or reject this information.

We repeat one more time that there exists a force called God, the all that is, our father and so on, that doesn't actually exist in any measurable fashion but, from somewhere, curiosity and collective consciousness does exist.

Once again, these are unmeasurable concepts. You can't see curiosity. You can't measure, weigh it or hold it in your hand. It is a concept, like God, that just exists. Therefore, if it just exists, it must exist in nothingness. Similarly, with collective consciousness, it is a concept, that just exists suspended in time and space - or rather outside of time and space. It just exists.

Now, curiosity is something we can understand. We all, or most of us, have curiosity. We break off for a moment to say that curiosity, one of the building blocks of life, has long since been a subject that the Archons have tried to suppress in humanity. After all, the Archons do not have curiosity, so they think that no one should have it. They just want the world's population to carry on as they are, never thinking, never questioning reality, never asking the question 'why'.
If they could prevent curiosity, they would have a better chance of maintaining their stranglehold over us for all eternity.
If we were curious, we might start to question religions, the political systems, the financial systems, the power system and so on.

That is why all religions have a holy book, which they claim comes from God, and effectively enslaves the adherents to that religion under pain of hell.
If people accept, without question, the teachings of their particular religion, they are assured of a place in heaven.
The slightest doubt as to the absolute truth of that religion, will assure a place in hell - for all eternity.
So, many people who adhere to a religion walk about like blind men - or perhaps we might even say, people with part of their brain missing - blindly believing information that a moment's thought would show to be false.
But to question a religion requires curiosity. Thus, if curiosity could be suppressed, the enslavement of the adherents is assured.

We could go on to discuss the other topics that we mentioned, but we leave it to you to question - or not - the life you lead, and you see around you.

We give you a warning, however. The leaders, often under the control of the Archons, take a dim view of questioning established systems, and will bite back hard if criticized so, question by all means, but keep your own counsel.

Do not cast pearls before swine.

Similar although different, is the strangely named collective conscious. Like curiosity, it exists, indeed, is an absolutely vital part of life as you know it but does not exist in any measurable form.

Therefore, if life exists at all, it exists as curiosity and collective conscious. It is stated in the Bible that God made everything in his image. Naturally, everything was narrowed down to just humans, and as humans seemed real, God was imagined to be a man with the attributes that elderly wise men had at that time; a beard, etc.

It never crossed anyone's mind to think that God might be an invisible, unknowable force, having just curiosity and collective consciousness as his attributes.

However, it is true that God made everything in his image, which is why all that exists is curiosity and collective consciousness.

Now, as we also said, we have all been programmed by Archangels to think this world we see around us, in all its dimensions and sub-dimensions, is real.

But, it is all created by imagination, which we will use as another way of explaining curiosity and collective consciousness.

The collective conscious works on all of us to imagine that we are real, and it is our imagination that creates all that our five senses; sight, hearing, taste, touch and smell, work to convince us that life is real, we are real and physicality is real.

So, we have this vast structure that seems multidimensional (that we have explored with you in various books) but, that is all just created by us thinking it is real, which gives us some idea of the power of imagination.

Now, what has all this got to do with aliens?

Quite simply, that aliens are a product of our imagination, just as everything else is.

But there is more to the story than that, obviously.

We mentioned at the beginning of this book about personalities, and although we did not mention the personalities of humans, because we had covered that subject in other works, and you, being human, can analyse your particular and general personality and speak for yourself, so we felt it unnecessary to elaborate further.

But it is important that you remember what we said about sub-dimensions and that all personality traits were contained in the sub-dimensions and, finally, the whole thing was repeated eight times in all the eight dimensions.

Now, this is where it is going to be extremely difficult to explain because, in fact, these personality traits that you have both individually and collectively, create entities beyond those that you are aware of that just apply to you.

It is almost as if these personality traits have got a sort of life, a consciousness of their own, and can think for themselves.

Can you see how difficult this is going to be to explain because, first we are dealing with personality traits, that most of you up till this moment did not know existed, and now we are saying that your, and everybody else's personality traits, create beings we call aliens. We hope that we will not confuse you too much, because we very much want you to have an understanding of this important subject - aliens - and so we are going to try to explain as slowly and carefully as we can.

Let us return to what we were explaining at the beginning of this book about personalities.
Indeed, it might be a good idea if you returned to the chapter about personalities to refresh your memory.
For those who want to stay with us, we will give a brief resumé.

We said that all things were alive and thus had personalities.
Then, we explained that for every atom of an object or creature, including humans, in the astral realms, there was a space, a channel, with the particular frequency of that object.

So, if we take a hypothetical person, you, us, or anyone, we have a number of channels created that correspond to that person's vibration.
Then, placed within those channels, are all the atoms that go to makeup that person.
So, in effect, there are countless millions of channels, all vibrating to someone's frequency, and the whole lot are linked together by gravitational force. And this is done for all people, all animals, all plants and all minerals.
The concept is staggering, but it is true.

Then, we said that, according to the species, and according to the individual, certain personality traits are formed within those channels, that can come forwards or retreat according to the species and the nature of the individual concerned.

Thus, we have to imagine that this hypothetical human is, using his ID, his collective conscious, and his other aspects that make him think he is a flesh and blood being, linking with his personality traits, and a human being appears either in the astral realms, or in physicality, if he has chosen to be born on Earth.

But, we also mentioned that all those personality traits were repeated eight times, even though the individual would be concentrating on only one aura at the time.
So, for most people, the other seven aspects of the human are not being used.

The person, whether he is in the heavenly spheres or in incarnation, is only concentrating on using one of his eight bodies at any one time.

But, the other seven auras do not lie idle. They have life and personalities. Normally they would be a close, almost identical reflection of the person who was using a particular aura.

But, they can start to think for themselves, because they are just as alive as the 'body' the person is concentrating on, so they have the same potential to react, to think, to create as the aura that is active.
This is a difficult concept to grasp, so we hope you will excuse us if we repeat this in other words.

Imagine a person, let us ignore his physical body and just imagine his non-physical aspects.
He would have ID, Higher Self, Imagination, mind, and a number of personality aspects all active. This person is only aware of one of him, as his focus is concentrated on one aspect of him, one version of him.

But, we said that he has another seven versions of him, that are there, but are not being used.
These other seven versions of him are also in touch with his Higher Self, Imagination, and all the same aspects as the 'person' is using.
The only difference, is that he is not using the other seven versions of himself.

So, these other seven versions have a choice.
They can either lie idle doing nothing, or they can take a decision to do something.
There are a number of things they could do, a number of avenues they could explore that do not concern us … except for one!
They could - or one of them could - decide to become what we term an alien for a while, whilst waiting to be called into action at some time.
Should that aura be called into action by the individual transferring his attention to the 'alien' aura, he will instantly drop the idea and return to being a human, either physical or non-physical.
Can you visualise this?

Now, not all auras of all humans decide to take independent action. Indeed, most people's auras are as asleep as the average person is, but we wish to stress that auras (versions of someone), are capable of taking independent action and, to gain experience, do one of a number of things, explore one of many avenues, and one of these avenues he could explore would be to become an alien.

Of course, the individual who has his focus concentrated on another of his auras, would have no idea that one of his auras was exploring a separate avenue to him.

This seems strange, but that is the truth of the matter.

What you call aliens, are just one of your - or someone else's – auras, playing at being an alien in order to gain experience and to stop being bored, although we are being light hearted about it.

We do appreciate that in the past, we have described a number of things about life which are new to you, and are very difficult to accept, but that this is the most outlandish of all.

So, we will repeat before going on to explain and explore the way that this alien phenomena operates.

An alien, is quite simply the aura of a person that is not being used by that person.

That is why some aliens seem good and kind, and some seem very nasty: they have the same, or virtually the same, personalities as the people who are incarnate or in the non-physical worlds.

Can we prove any of this? The answer is no, no more than we could really prove to you that you have auras at all, any more than we could demonstrate to you that angels or demons are real.

However, before we stated what we have just revealed to you, you can be sure that we took the utmost care to verify with our angelic helpers that this was, and is, the truth.

We would not make such extravagant claims, unless we were, ourselves, utterly assured that this is the case.

So, we do apologise if we shocked you, and you feel that we are mocking you as, no doubt, some people will feel.
We can only ask you either to accept what we are saying or dismiss it, if it sounds too far-fetched for you, or put it at the back of your mind until someone finds a way to verify our statement.

In the meantime, we will go on and discuss other aspects of this topic for the rest of this book.

CHAPTER 9

AN INTRODUCTION TO ALIENS - PART 3

So, let us start to delve into what exactly aliens are, (although we gave an overview earlier), and explain how their craft and their robots are constructed, and manage to appear in, and on, planet Earth and in its skies.

We will also, in this book, try to establish the link between so-called aliens, and 'experiencers', although we rather feel that all this will be somewhat difficult to accept for many people, especially those who have, or are, building careers for themselves, describing their experiences and their versions of what aliens are.

As you can imagine, the story is rather complicated to explain, so we will take our time and use a number of chapters to describe each aspect of alien life and how it affects us - or rather you - incarnate.

Naturally, as most of this will be new to most - if not all - of you, we do not expect all of you to be able to accept our version and, no doubt, much of our tale will be dismissed by established 'experts' who, if they accepted our version, would see their careers crash down like a house of cards so, many people - even those we know who voraciously read our books and essays, and hunt for ways and means of incorporating our version of life's events into their books and lectures - will ignore most of what we are going to say.
After all, what we have already said and what we are going to tell you, would have the greatest difficulty in being incorporated into stories that aliens come from various planets, meet regularly with certain specially selected humans, and are given secret information, thus entitling those special people to charge fees giving lectures, selling books and revealing the alien's agendas and secrets.

We feel that we are going to cause a rift in accepted ufology by what we are going to say, and people will have to make a decision to believe them, or us.
Who they finally decide to put their weight behind is not our concern.
We have been informed by knowledgeable Archangels of what the story concerning so-called aliens is, and we present it to you. In a way, our responsibility stops there.
It has been our experience that much of what we tell you is largely ignored until, little by little, person by person, others begin to accept the wisdom behind what we tell you and the truth spreads.

We are not interested in instant sensationalism. That which we tell you is intended to fill library shelves - and the computers of many people - for generations to come, as truths today will still be true long years into the future.

So, accept what you can, reject what you cannot, but please do not let any of our revelations upset or anger you. We come in peace, and present, with love, the truth as we know it to be, to you, and leave it in your hands to accept or reject this information.

Indeed, it may come as a relief to some to know that what they seemed to experience at the hands of aliens may not have happened quite as they visualised it.

Even in hypnotic regression, we hope to demonstrate that what people re-experience may not be quite so dramatic as it seems.

So, like all good tales, or most, we start with the phrase, 'Let us begin'.

The problem is that this story is going to be so new, so revolutionary to most people, that we feel we should return to the last chapter, where we mentioned that aliens are actually versions of people in auric dimensions, and expand on that theme until, we hope, you all have an absolutely clear picture of what we were describing.

Now, we may need to branch away from strict scientific fact concerning aliens in order to make the picture clear, but the Master Jesus set the precedent by often creating stories - analogies - to explain difficult concepts, so we will be standing on the shoulders of a spiritual giant if we do the same. Our object is that you should understand as clearly as we can explain just what aliens are, and their connection to us both incarnate and discarnate.

There is no point in going too far back in the story of personalities, and the fact that they are repeated eight times, because we have done our utmost to describe them in previous chapters and, if you haven't understood that, nothing more we can add will clarify the situation.

So, we will assume that you have understood that you have a number of personality aspects, and each group of these personality aspects is held together in a bundle by gravity, and this bundle of personality aspects is repeated seven more times, making eight personality bundles in all.

Further, all of these bundles are capable of making contact with your Higher Self, Imagination, ID, and all the rest that goes up to make you.

We should perhaps add, in case we did not make this quite clear, that not only can each bundle, individually, make contact with his outside elements of you; Higher Self, Imagination, ID, etc., but they could all do this at the same time, although you would not be aware of more than one bundle making contact at a time. This would be the bundle of personality aspects that you are using at the moment, as you go through your incarnation and are reading this book.

So, we repeat. You, who are sitting reading this book with, apparently physical eyes, struggling to comprehend with your physical brain have, working in the background, a number of personality aspects, some more strongly present than others, and all these personality aspects are working in conjunction with your Higher Self, Imagination, ID, and a number of other features that we have already mentioned in previous works, and the whole lot is focused in what you see as your physical body.

You are only aware that you have one of you - the one who is reading this book - but you have exactly the same complex repeated another seven times, making eight of you in all. The reason, actually, why you cannot see or feel all eight of you, is that each bundle of personality aspects is on different frequencies, rather as if you had a computer with eight identical programs running, but all kept separate by being on different carrier waves.

So, you focus just on one aspect of you (your personality bundle). As we said, there is only one Higher Self, one Imagination, and one ID, so all the eight bundles share those just mentioned attributes. It is only the personality bundles, that there are eight of, that are independent.

We hope that you have now fully understood this concept because;
a. Without using diagrams, we could not describe the concept with greater clarity, and;
b. If you have not understood, you will never understand what aliens are.

We went on to explain that these personality bundles are, in conjunction with using the Higher Self, Imagination, ID, etc., capable of independent thought, just as you are. Indeed, if you were capable of splitting your attention into eight, you would see eight of you, although each one would be of a different frequency. Perhaps it is just as well that you can't divide your attention into eight, because it might prove to be somewhat confusing! Most people have enough trouble handling one aspect of life. Nevertheless, on different frequencies, your other seven versions of you are just as capable of independent thought and action as you are.

Therefore, these other aspects of you could do a number of things, one of which is to explore life in another dimension, and we call them, when they interact with us… aliens.

We must stress, that all of your seven other auras would be on other frequencies, and so, if one did, indeed, decide to become what we term an alien, it would be totally invisible to our eyes, and even to UV or infrared light, being of a frequency far removed from so-called physicality.

That is why we can state categorically, that anyone who claims to see or interact with aliens is mistaken. They are quite invisible to us.

Also, we must say that each bundle of personalities has its own unique frequency, and thus would be invisible to the personality bundle of anyone else. Each and every person has their own unique frequency.
Thus, if a personality bundle of one person decided to become an alien, that person would be alone. If a second person decided to become an alien he would be invisible to the first alien.

We have already stated in other works that each person is totally alone in reality because each person has a unique frequency.
Thus, if someone claims to have attended a meeting where there were a number of aliens, he might see robots, PLFs, but in no way would he be looking at aliens.

Perhaps we should also say that these personality bundles, when they are wandering about the astral realms, are not considered to be aliens.
That appellation only applies to them, their craft, and their robots, when they decide to interact with us.

The astral realms contain countless personality bundles wandering about completely unknown to humans.
Perhaps we will write a paper about this aspect of life, should it prove to be interesting to people.
But, it is only when they interact with us that we call them aliens.

Therefore, we have a strange phenomenon. People's unused personality bundles can, if they wish, wander about quite independently of each other, and of the person incarnate, or discarnate, who is completely unaware that this is occurring.
Of all this vast number, only a relatively few actually have the curiosity to try to contact the surface of planet Earth, and then go about manufacturing UFOs and robots - a subject which, obviously, we will deal with in depth later.

But, we must mention another strange effect of auras - which is what these bundles of personalities are usually referred to.

You may remember that, earlier, we gave a little story about a young girl, and her various dolls, and we mentioned that these personality bundles, these auras, always stay with the person.
And now we are saying that they can wander about on their own.
So, is this not a problem? How can an aura be attached, or close to a person, and yet wander about independently of the person at the same time?
Surely, it must be one or the other, although, we did qualify things by saying that there was nothing stopping an aura wandering off if it chose?

This is where higher physics comes in.
We have stated, in past works, that neither time nor space actually exist, it is part of the great illusion on Earth, and is associated with the fight/flight aspect of life.

In the astral realms, there is no physical danger, thus fight/flight is not necessary, and thus, time/space does not exist.
There is only the 'now' moment, and only 'here'.

Therefore, a personality bundle (the personality aura of someone), can appear to be wandering about, but attached to the Earthly aspect of someone at the same time.

We will also say that not everyone's personality aspects (or bundles), are capable of operating independently of the controlling spirit, that is to say a human incarnate or discarnate.
It is a question of a number of things.

There are some people who are not very intelligent. This is not a criticism but just a fact. If a person lacks intelligence, it implies that his personalities have only a very limited ability to contact the Higher Self, and thus he appears to have limited intelligence, because intelligence implies knowledge and wisdom, which, is contained in the Higher Self - the source of all knowledge and wisdom.

So, if a person cannot really make contact with the Higher Self, the various personality aspects would have a distinct lack of curiosity, and thus it is unlikely that any one of that person's personality aspects (bundles), would really be active.

Then there are those that are deeply involved in any of the major religions.
In this case, those people would only have limited personality aspects developed, and curiosity about real life is unlikely to be present.

Then there are those who, for various reasons, do not wish to admit that aliens are a real possibility and so, for them, their spare personality bundles would not desire to become aliens.

So, to cut a long story short, it would be the personality aspects of reasonably intelligent, open minded people, who would create aliens.

Now, of this group who might become what we referred to as aliens, some of these people might be very kind, loving people, and some might be extremely nasty, egocentric, cruel people - or a whole range in between, just as there is on Earth.

You can be sure that if you happen to meet someone, male or female, who is very kind, and if one of their personality bundles decided to explore the avenue of what we call an alien, that alien would also be a kind, loving, being.

Equally, of course, an evil person would tend to create an evil alien.
The ones in the middle (the vast amount of people), would just create aliens with no particular agenda, just aliens that would observe life from their point of view without taking sides.

Maybe, we can see where reports of good, bad, and indifferent aliens come from. They are all personality aspects of people, either incarnate or discarnate.

There is, however, one particularly negative group, the PLFs of whom you know as Grey's. This group merit a short chapter of their own, and so we will discuss them later.

The question has been asked, as to whether the personality aspects of any animals - for animals have eight aspects to them just as humans have - could become aliens, but animals, generally, lack curiosity, so it would not be likely that the spare personality bundles of any animal would desire to wander off on their own, and even more unlikely that it would desire to come close to Earth as an alien.

So, to wrap up this particular chapter, we will resume what we have said about the various life forms you know as aliens.

There are very few races that are closely connected to humanity, one of which we call either the Tall Whites or the Nordics, who are true, living people, just as you are, but who live apart from you.

Then there are the personality bundles of some people who choose to come close to Earth, interact with Earth and, sometimes, it's population. Of this group some are good, some are not good, and most are indifferent.

And then there is this group known as the Grey's.

Of all these various life forms, only the Tall Whites have physical bodies as you have. All the rest live in the astral realms and are invisible to humanity.
It is only their manufactured UFOs and PLFs that are directly observable to humans.

CHAPTER 10

ALIENS & PLFs

Where in this complex topic should we turn next, to try to unravel the mysteries surrounding the different aspects of ufology and its apparent interaction with mankind?

Before we make a decision, we feel it would be beneficial if we examined somewhat Egyptology, from the point of view of the many and beautifully made paintings and statues, apparently depicting weird and wonderful creatures, sometimes with the bodies of animals with human heads and sometimes the other way around.

For instance, these paintings and statues of people with hawk like heads, has been seized on by some lecturers to invent bird like aliens.
Should anyone doubt the veracity of their claims, they point to these depictions as proof that aliens with bird's heads exist.
Similarly, people claim to be in touch with aliens with human bodies and cat like heads - the opposite to a Sphinx in a way.

We hope that you can understand from what we have written earlier, that this is just make believe. We repeat, true aliens live in the sub-dimensions of the astral realms, and even if they were to create PLFs, it is very doubtful that they would bother to spend a vast amount of energy creating birdman or catman, when they already have an adequate range of PLFs, the blueprints of which were created many long years in the past and who serve their needs adequately.

No one, not even aliens, wastes energy - with the possible exception of man incarnate! Anyone in the astral realms would be only too aware of the vast amount of psychic (auric) energy that would go into creating a PLF and so, unless it was strictly necessary, an alien would not waste that energy.

So, is it possible to examine the depictions of strange creatures found in or close to ancient pharaonic structures and decipher what they depict, and any possible connection to ufology?

Now, we will say straight away that aliens have been visiting Earth - or rather, the PLFs have - since man developed sufficient awareness and curiosity to wish to explore.

This goes back an extremely long time, because, we would like you to remember that man has come and gone many times over the long history of Earth and so, as aliens are just unused personality aspects, and as life has always followed the same pattern of construction, we can say with certainty, that alien's interest in Earth dates back a very long time indeed.

This latest "civilisation", the one you are currently in, is fairly recent. We will not mention dates, because we do not wish to open the door for any archaeologist or historian to defend his sacred territory by attacking any date. But we assure you that the history of man, and thus alien visitations, dates back a long way into the past.

So, what can we say about Egypt?

We have mentioned the construction of the pyramids and have said that they were planned by a group of aliens we called the builder race.
We will discuss this race and how they communicated later.

Thus, we know that aliens were in contact with Earth a mere 15,000 years ago, which is about the time that the main pyramids of Giza, and in other parts of the world, were constructed.

However, none of the pharaonic sites date back even that far, so all the depictions of strange beings are much younger.

Where did the idea of these creatures come from? After all, to do a painting of a creature with a mixture of man and beast (or bird) features takes a lot of skill and energy. To create statues of similar objects in hard stone would take even longer and require much more effort, so logic dictates that the Egyptians must have had good reason to make them.

The simple truth is that all this has nothing to do with aliens.
They, the Egyptians, developed a very extensive priest caste and, of course, there were those that appointed themselves to be rulers - pharaohs.
Now, to be a pharaoh gave one almost God-like status.
So, the priests were instructed to create ways and means of depicting the God like status of the pharaohs in art.

We must also mention hallucinatory drugs in relation to this art.
The Egyptians created, or developed, a range of drugs, some of which were used as medicine, such as marijuana, which grew easily in the Egyptian climate and, very probably, were survivors of the climatic change brought about at the time of a catastrophic event recorded in many old books as the great flood.
Before then, Egypt was in a much more tropical zone than it is today, so a number of plants grew in that hot, damp climate.

So, much of the narcotics that we know of today were available at that time and people took freely of them.
There was also a form of Ayahuasca.
This drug creates illusions in the mind and the user of that drug imagines all sorts of weird and wonderful creatures.

So, the priests and artists took various drugs and visualised strange beings, which seemed so real, sometimes, that they thought that they were in touch with Gods.

Thus, it all came together nicely.

The Pharaoh wanted statues and paintings depicting his God-like status, the priests and artists, under the influence of hallucinogenic drugs, visualized strange creatures that they thought might be Gods, and thus images of what was imagined became artwork, much of which still survives to this day, and is used to create the myth of alien creatures.

They were, actually, the result of egocentric pharaohs, then priests and artists, using drugs to create with their imaginations, images which they persuaded the pharaoh was his spiritual representation of his God-like status, despite what his physical body might have looked like after years of excessive eating, drinking, drug taking and the other pleasures of the flesh.

But history has left us some remarkable artwork, so we should be grateful for the system that came together to allow skilled artists to create the images.

However, we should not confuse what we see in the art with any factual events. The artwork is all allegorical.

Having got that subject out of the way, we return to the aliens.

Perhaps the first subject we could discuss, is how aliens seem to contact each other. We mentioned this builder race so, perhaps, it would be appropriate if we combined methods of communication with what the builder race decided to do.

Now, the answer to the first subject is easy. It is telepathy. You may be aware that those who live in non-physicality cannot talk to each other using sound waves as you do, because in the astral realms, air, as you know it, does not exist. One could say that non-physical beings live in a vacuum, but that would not be true.

However, if you know that sound waves cannot travel in a vacuum, that will do as an example.

Thus, all non-physical entities communicate telepathically, or rather, by thought.

We are reluctant to delve once again into a long explanation of how thought transference works, but please accept that what is termed telepathy, is thought transference.

Now, we said earlier that each person actually lives in isolation, and it is only imagination and collective consciousness that gives the impression that we are surrounded by other people.

These personality bundles, that wander about, are no different than us - they are us - so, they too can use imagination, to pretend that they are in contact with other life form personality bundles and, using telepathy, can communicate under certain circumstances.

We will just touch on the builder race at this moment because, what we will say about them will equally apply to all personality bundles, regardless of whether they decide to become aliens or not.

We wish you to clearly understand, that everything that applies to you, applies to your other seven unused personality aspects.
The only difference is that the particular aspect of you that you have your concentration on, has been programmed to imagine that you have a physical body and are living on a physical world, whereas the other seven aspects of you have not been programmed in this manner.
Thus, the only real difference is that you have one personality bundle that thinks it is physical, and seven others that are aware that they are not physical.
In fact, the part of you that thinks you are physical, has nothing to do with your personality aspects. The part that has been programmed to think that it is physical is connected both to your ID and to imagination. So, all eight of your personality bundles are quite independent of your sense of physicality but, of course, your sense of being physical will bring aspects of personality forward, that the other seven aspects would not give importance to.
Fight/flight is an obvious example.
It is important in physicality to be ready to defend oneself from danger, but that danger does not exist in that form outside of physicality.

Thus, the personality bundle that you use whilst incarnate would not be quite the same as the personality bundles contained in association with the other seven "you's".

You will have the basic make-up of who you are - a good person or a less than good person - present in all eight personality traits, but there will be variations according to how the eight different "you's" decide to explore life.

We do apologise for having promised to talk about aliens, and yet we seem to be wandering all over the place, describing or repeating matters that do not seem to be connected to aliens.
However, it is necessary that you completely understand how life works, whether physical or alien, or we would have failed in our task of explaining aliens to you.

For instance, we could have said quite simply that aliens are "aspects of you", but we hope that you would agree that it would not have been very helpful in your understanding really of what aliens are.

As it is, life is far more complex than what we have stated in any of our books or lessons, and we hope, in future books, to explain more about the intricacies of life, so we have deliberately chosen to give you, so far, a simplified version of life. To try to give you the full picture in one go would just baffle you so we need to reveal information a bit at a time.

We think that many of you are already struggling to comprehend what we have given you so far, so you can appreciate that it would be pointless in delving too deeply at the moment.

To understand the basic philosophy of aliens, it is sufficient to understand that the seven unused versions of you are able to think and to act independently, and some of those aspects of you might choose to interact with life on Earth, and we term such aspects aliens.

So, all we will say about the builder race at this time, is that all personality bundles can, using Higher Self, Imagination, etc., contact and visualise other personality bundles, rather as you can contact and visualise other people on Earth, and thus can work together.

Just like people in incarnation, these aliens have different and diverse interests. They do not think the same at all like ants and bees - with the exception of the Grey's whom, we said we would discuss later, as they do not quite fit into the general picture of what aliens are.

Now, regarding the builder race, to describe them in detail would take us on to a point where we would be getting ahead of ourselves, because this group were formed to solve the problems of navigating around the physical galaxy, so we would need to explain about UFOs before talking about the builder race, but we wish to say this.
Just like all of us, personality bundles are every bit as alive as we are and, like us, have varying interests.

Therefore, when it became obvious that some form of navigation device was necessary to help space faring aliens find their way around the galaxy, this group, who shared a similar interest in construction navigation beacons, was formed between like-minded aliens (personality bundles), and applied themselves to resolving how to construct navigation beacons.

You must be tired by now of us talking about personality bundles, and not really talking about aliens as you know them, so let us begin to examine the little bug eyed beings variously known as aliens - which they are not - programmed life forms, PLF, Grey's, robots, etc.

We repeat for the last time, that the true group known as the Grey's, are a different species in a way, but as most PLFs, whatever group make them, look somewhat similar, these little robot forms are often lumped together and just called a Grey.

Now, it must be obvious to you that in the case of humans, who incarnate as you are now, you are in two parts; the spiritual or non-physical part, and the physical part - your body. You should also know by now that your body is not actually alive, it is the non-physical part that animates the physical part and directs it as it wanders about on Earth.

Once again, there is more to the process than that, and we have attempted in various books to explain how the system works but, if we simplify things to the basic processes, we have just two aspects; the spirit or non-physical part controlling a physical robot - your body.

Thus, we hope that you can see that those personality aspects that decide to interact with planet Earth, and its people, needed something similar as they - the so-called aliens - would not be able directly to appear on the surface, any more than your spirit or non-physical aspect could.
So, they took a page from our book, so to speak, and decided to try to create roughly the equivalent of our physical body.
The main difference being that our physical body needs to have quite a large degree of both intelligence and autonomy to be able to survive for a complete incarnation here on Earth, with all its trials and tribulations, whereas the alien personalities only needed a basic creature capable of following a few simple orders telepathically.

It is interesting to note that, in a way, the human body is following orders from the spirit part, using a form of telepathy, which is why telepathy can be learnt by humans - indeed all life - their being no direct link between the spiritual or non-physical aspect of living things and the physical part. There is a constant stream of telepathic commands being issued by the spirit and being received by the body, which simply implements the commands of the spirit.

Thus, the personality aspect that decides to become an alien simply has to copy what already existed.

As we have said, into these PLF, robots, certain skills were programmed: the ability to walk, follow orders, change frequency to become invisible (in certain cases, not all), and to transmit impressions of what they might be interacting with back to the alien using telepathy.
But, the overall intelligence installed would be, in our terms, an IQ of about 80, which, in a human would be considered almost imbecility, if you forgive us for using that unpleasant sounding word. Once again, we do not wish to get into a debate about exactly what level of IQ merits the word imbecile. The point we wish to make is that they have just enough intelligence to obey commands, but not sufficient to start to think for themselves.
If a PLF decided to take life into its own hands, as has been portrayed in at least one feature film (a comedy), and the aliens in the astral realm lost control of it, the aliens would have no means of recuperating it.
Thus, these PLF are given just enough intelligence to obey orders and that is all.

Now, we noticed that dogs seem to be very similar to that, but dogs are quite intelligent. But, generally, they have great love, or fear, for their masters, and so subjugate their desires to the will of the master.
That requires intelligence, and we have great respect and love for dogs, man's faithful friend and ally over long years.

We mentioned dogs because those who have seen sheep dogs herding a flock of sheep, will have noticed the shepherd stands and watches the flock of sheep, and issues commands either verbally or with whistles to the dog or dogs, who recognise the sounds and translate them into commands to do something: run left, run right, lie down or whatever.

If the shepherd has his dogs under his total control, the sheep finish up in the pen or enclosure, and the shepherd proudly closes the gate to the applause of the watching crowd.

With PLF, we have an almost identical situation. Let us take the example of an abduction. The spacecraft appears (the equivalent of the sheep pen), and the PLF are told, telepathically, to walk out and abduct some human or humans into the craft.

The PLFs are constantly receiving orders to do this or that and if all goes well, from the alien point of view, the humans are introduced into the spacecraft. It is a very similar procedure to what a shepherd does.

Now, let us try to find out how a PLF is made.

The aliens, a long time ago, created a plan for the little creatures they needed, and based it on the human form. Thus, it has a head, body, two arms, two legs, eyes, and that is about all, except for a brain, of course.

The brain operates in two parts.

There is the part that receives the telepathic commands from the alien who, we remind you, always stays in the astral realms, and the second part of the brain, which controls the motor functions of the PLF.

The eyes are actually cameras, sending back to the alien images in stereo of what the PLF appears to be looking at.

In fact, the PLF cannot see. It doesn't need to. The alien sees and directs operations.

Now, the PLF appears to have no ears. Once again it doesn't need them.

The alien master is able to pick up the telepathic thoughts of any human that the PLF interacts with, and so is able to anticipate any resistance on behalf of the human.

It has been suggested that PLFs have extreme telepathic skills, but this is not the case at all. It is the alien in the astral realms that can link telepathically with the astral form of a human and can thus react instantly to any thoughts that the human might have.

So how is the body made? Humans have, nowadays, bodies made of flesh and blood, although, as we have said, it was not always the case.

Many, many millions of years ago, an experiment was conducted to try to make animals, at least, of plants. We explained that this experiment failed. So, eventually, flesh and blood creatures and humans were invented, and we still have that model today.

People seldom question where the flesh and blood body comes from. What makes it?

After all, many people are strict vegetarians and only eat vegetables, fruit, etc., but that vegetable matter is, by some miracle, transformed into flesh and blood.

The fact of the matter is that everything is astral matter and vibrates.
There is actually no such thing as vegetables nor meat.
All that exists is astral in nature.
But we live in this imagined world created by Archangels, and so we appear to have bodies made of flesh.
It is actually astral matter, the frequency of which is altered until it appears in our physical world as physical matter.

Of course, many of you will be questioning this, as we said that in reality nothing exists in physical form but let us go along with the "grand illusion" and pretend that physicality does exist.

Therefore, you are made of astral matter, the frequency of which is altered until it looks like flesh.
So, these aliens did much the same. They took astral matter, molded it around the form that they had astrally created (the little PLF form), altered the frequency and we have a PLF - a programmed life form.

Now, we wish to make two points concerning the PLFs, one of which we mentioned earlier.
Autopsies of PLF corpses have revealed a certain amount of vegetable matter within them.
Now, we cannot be certain of this, but we are of the opinion that this vegetable matter dates back to the days when the Archangels tried to introduce animals made of plant life - which failed.

So, we think that a PLF dates back to those days - or the plan for them does - and at some point, was updated when flesh was created.

The second point is that these PLF are only created while the spaceship is in 3D reality.
A spaceship (UFO), actually comes from an astral realm - as we will explain soon - and enters our 3D reality, at which point it appears solid.
The PLF, when in astral form, are only a concept.
When the UFO transfers to 3D reality, not only does the UFO appear solid, but the PLFs also appear as you see them.
But, that solidity only lasts until they return to the astral realms. Then it disappears.
Solid, physical forms, cannot be in astral realms.

Now, let us examine the power source of a PLF. The energy that gives it the ability to operate in a 3D realm.
From what we just mentioned above, once back in the astral realms, it only exists as a concept. But, as soon as the UFO, which transports PLFs to our 3D world, appears in our reality, the physical body is put on the astral form, so to speak, and a PLF appears as a solid moving creature.
So, this physical form obviously needs to have a power source.

Now, once again we return to the human form.

We are of the opinion that our energy comes from the food we eat and, in a way, this is true because, if someone is deprived of food for long enough, he or she will expire.

So, food seems essential.

But, it is not actually the food that contains the fuel that keeps us going, it is the astral energy contained in association with food that acts as fuel for us.

So, what the aliens have done, is to devise a way of taking that astral energy directly from the cosmos, and allowing that astral energy to act as fuel for a PLF.

As we have already explained, it would be possible for us humans to do the same, but evolution has designed us to eat and digest food, and it is the bacteria in our intestines that break down the food, extract the spiritual energy, and we reject the rest as waste. We have to respect that system or we become unwell.

But PLF, somehow - we are not exactly sure how it is done - extract the energy directly from the cosmos.

The problem we have in understanding how this is achieved is as follows.

We have mentioned that the Archangels, long before you were born, created enough atoms to sustain you throughout your incarnation.

We explain this at length and refer you to the appropriate chapter if you do not understand.

But a PLF is not alive. It is a machine - a robot. It does not eat, it does not breathe. Some, not all, have a rudimentary heart, but it serves no real purpose.

So, unless the Archangels anticipated that PLF would come to Earth, and put certain atoms containing energy expressly for them in the atmosphere, we are somewhat at a loss to know what mechanism permits them to absorb energy.

Some people have said that they eat by creating a sort of paste from animal products and smearing it on their skin and excrete in a similar method, but it is pure fantasy.

PLF do not eat in any recognisable form nor do they excrete.

You will find no kitchens or bathrooms on UFOs!

They are machines and are powered rather as machines are.

However, like all machines, they are mindless and neutral as regards emotions. They are not capable of independent thought, nor of making any decisions. They obey orders. If told to stand still, for instance, they would remain on that spot forever. If told to perform any action, they would do that unceasingly just like any machine would.

So, if someone had a genuine encounter with aliens, and experienced all the paralysis or powerlessness that one experiences, or abducted people often mention, they should not blame the PLF.

A PLF would be no more capable of performing any independent action than an automobile would.
The driver of a car may decide to take certain actions but the car just obeys the driver's orders.

We have so far concentrated our attention on the small robots generally referred to as Grey's but the same would apply to any alien creature.
Whether it would be a praying mantis looking creature, or any other shaped object aliens might invent, they would all be simple machines, and one should not be frightened of them.
They will not harm a person. Virtually all of them have no weapons, and certainly would not be capable of deciding when to use one, even if it were armed.

They do not have very great physical strength and could easily be overpowered by even a large child.
The reason that they so easily abduct people, is that fear persuades most people to think that they are powerless in the face of this "vastly superior alien force" and that, combined with a degree of mind control projected by the personality bundle, who are the true aliens, is sufficient to breakdown any resistance.

If we return to the description we presented to you earlier of the shepherd pushing sheep into a pen, it is very similar. If we imagine the shepherd to be the alien, the dogs to be the PLFs and the sheep to be the people, the dogs are trained never, physically, to attack the sheep.
So, if the sheep wanted, the shepherd could issue instructions until he was blue in the face, the dogs could chase about until they ran out of steam, but if the sheep decided to ignore the dogs, they could carry on munching grass peacefully.
But they don't.
As soon as the dogs appear, flight/flight - or rather, in the case of sheep, just flight - kicks in and so the shepherd has control over them.

It is a very similar situation with the alien scenario. It is only fear that gives these PLF power over a human.

The personality bundle (alien), actually has very limited ability to influence a person any more than a shepherd has power directly to influence sheep.
The PLF do not have any physical or psychic power to influence humans, any more than a trained sheepdog has power to influence sheep in a competition, and yet, abductions are just as easily performed on humans as control of the sheep is produced.
It is fear that enables that. It is also a form of illusion, just as a power of the dogs over sheep is an illusion.

We will discuss abductions and interactions with aliens later, but we wish to say this.
In the unlikely event that you actually find yourself in the presence of these little Grey PLFs, do not give in to fear. Realise that these PLF, with their strange appearance, have

actually no more independent thought than a modern washing machine, and you do not have to obey them.

If we imagine a scenario where you might be driving along a road, and then you see a UFO appear, and your car stops (which is caused by the electrical power of the UFO interfering with the electrical circuits of the car) and suddenly little PLF appear, you do not have to be frightened of them.
If you could realise that they have almost zero ability to do anything, any more than a washing machine would be able to interfere with you, you can resist them.

Of course, they will continue to try to abduct you because that was the last order they received, and so they will continue endlessly to try to take control of you.

So, at this point you have a few choices:
1. Either to comply with them and let them abduct you,
2. Physically repulse the PLF, damage them if you have any weapons available - not guns or knives, just anything you may have handy,
3. Send a telepathic message to the personality bundle that is in the astral realms directing operations, telling him/her/it to stop.

Now, these so-called aliens are not used to being opposed, and so you may have a bit of a tug of war with them before they realise that you have won, at which point the whole thing will return to the astral realms, and you may continue your journey.

Alien abductions are actually very rare but, should you find yourself in that unpleasant situation, remember what we told you about the shepherd and his sheep, and it is only fear that gives control to the shepherd.
Do not become frightened. Remember that you are actually in control and you will be left alone - unless, of course, you want to be abducted.

There are a surprising number of people who want to feel special and will do all sorts of things to achieve that end.

So, if an abduction scenario was to occur to any such person, they might be terrified, but would go along with the abduction, knowing that they are now special and could possibly write a book about their abduction, creating in their minds multiple abductions and, once the book published, tour the UFO circuit giving lectures to ordinary people to explain just how special they are with all the operations they have endured, all the infants they might have produced, etc.

Now, we are not belittling genuine people who happen to be in the wrong place at the wrong time, only that we do suggest that the UFO community should be very sceptical of the growing number of people who claim to have been abducted.

Before we think of bringing this chapter to a close, and moving onto another aspect of ufology, might we mention once more the little PLF generally depicted as grey in colour with huge wrap around eyes (which are actually filters placed over the eyes because, as we said, the eyes are actually cameras and filters are often placed over the lenses of cameras to protect the optics from bright sun).

If you think about it, your eyes are actually camera optics. They let images into the optics (eyes), which are converted into images in the brain, and people often wear dark glasses to protect their eyes from bright sunlight.

So, a PLF has a very similar system to humans.

Also, the skin colour varies somewhat according to whoever created the PLF. Some are grey, some are brown.

It depends on the material used to create the skin.

Now, we do realise that we have not covered all aspects of what aliens are, and what PLF are, but we have given a fairly in-depth overview, and so we will move on to discuss UFOs.

We have already noted a number of questions have been formulated, and so we will try to answer some throughout this book and create a sort of question and answer section at the end which, we hope, will be beneficial to explaining other matters which are of interest, but do not merit complete chapters of their own.

CHAPTER 11

UFOs – REAL & FALSE

In this chapter, we will examine the objects sometimes seen in the skies and are sometimes referred to as flying saucers, or unidentified flying objects (UFOs).

Now, there is some reason as to why they were originally referred to as flying saucers, because they did resemble somewhat a saucer skimming through the sky.

Unidentified flying objects is a little more vague, however.
Although it appears to be an object, once one has identified it as coming from somewhere else, it is not really unidentified, clearly being not of human incarnate manufacture.
We hope you realise also that, although it is in the sky, it is not really flying in the sense that a bird or even an aeroplane would. So, it is hardly a UFO.

However, you may remember when we started to discuss aliens, we had some difficulty in the nomenclature, but settled for aliens.

Similarly, we must call the spaceships something and we will settle for UFO.

So, what can we say about UFOs?
We might question why they exist, as a personality bundle that decides to become an alien would be quite capable of approaching Earth, and Earth humans in an astral sense, so would not really need a ship to get here.
Space in the astral world does not exist as it does in physicality so, providing the personality aspect contented itself with remaining in the astral realms, it could explore anywhere to its heart's content.
But physicality would be barred from it's experience.

We remind you once again that all people and all things, past, present and future have eight personality aspects but only one is programmed by Archangels to experience physicality, the other seven remaining in pure astral form.

Therefore, should one personality aspect decide to take the plunge to explore planet Earth, logic would dictate that it would need some means of navigating around the Earth or any other part of the physical universe for that matter.
Thus, the little robot creatures needed to be constructed and flying machines also constructed as the personality bundle must always remain in an astral dimension.

We should perhaps apologise for using the somewhat uncouth appellation 'personality bundle' to describe a living, thinking aspect of life, but we don't have a word to express the concept. So, out of desperation we chose that term because, in effect, that is what it is - a bundle of personality aspects held together by gravity and using some of the collective aspects we all share; Higher Self, Imagination, etc.

The alien, being stuck in the astral realms, needed something that would act as his eyes and ears while exploring the physical world and thus invented PLFs.
But to get the PLF here into physicality, it required a means of transport. So, UFOs were invented.

We mentioned earlier that it is our opinion that the plan for PLFs was created many millions of years ago, long before modern man came on the scene.
But, no doubt, millions of years ago, life was on planet Earth and has been eliminated and reborn countless times following disasters.
UFOs, however, were untouched by disasters as were the life forms we term aliens.
Astral life is largely unaffected by Earthly catastrophes.

So, once a basic plan for a flying machine was created, it could be modified, updated and improved, but would never be wiped out, being astral in form.

You should also know that, just to consider humanity, it is immortal. Once the physical body dies, the person with his eight personalities intact, soldiers on in the astral planes. Thus man, perhaps having a somewhat different physical form to today, but having the same astral form, has been around for a very long time.

The exact time is of no importance but let us say for the sake of understanding what we are trying to describe, 100 million years.

Had man the ability to live peacefully here on Earth for that length of time, try to imagine the advances in science he would have made.

So, if we can realise that man in his astral form is every bit as alive as he might be in physicality - more so, in fact - can you imagine the scientific wonders he has created in the astral realms?

You do not need for something to be physical to exist. After all, everything starts off as a thought, an idea, and it is only the final stages that become physical.

So, in the astral realms there are some stupendous inventions using concepts light years ahead of what is on Earth at the moment, even in the most advanced secret laboratories.

That is why the first crashed UFOs, when examined by man, completely baffled them.
If you think back, electronics in the 1940's was still very primitive using glass tubes (valves) to power radios, etc., whereas, when the interior of a UFO was examined, there was nothing recognisable to scientists of the day.

It is true to say that even today, although man incarnate has manufactured some flying craft using back engineered UFO technology, he has barely scratched the surface of the technology of a true UFO and will not for a long time into the future.

It has been suggested that science has developed so quickly due to back engineering downed UFOs and by using the assistance of PLFs, that aliens are only a few years ahead but the truth is that alien technology is far, far ahead.

The only technology that is released to man is just sufficient to keep a dialogue going between the Grey's and man.

Modern man would be quite incapable of understanding UFO technology, any more than a caveman could have understood how a modern aircraft flies.

You must understand that science has been developing in the astral realms continuously for a vast period of time. Then add to that the fact that each person who "dies" is actually eightfold, so you can imagine the vast army of people who have been developing all sorts of fields of interest continuously because, in the astral realms, we are not distracted by the hundred and one things that people incarnate have to deal with: working, eating, sleeping, house cleaning, walking the dog, shopping and so on.

We do not become fatigued in the astral realms, so can work endlessly on a project that interest us, so we advance at a great pace compared to man incarnate.

So, let us look in detail at a UFO, and see if we can understand how it works.

We wish you to understand, that anything that we mentioned is occurring in the astral, non-physical realms but, when we are in one of those realms, it seems just as solid and real to us as physicality does to you.

So, if we manufacture something, it looks like a solid object to us. But we do not have to cut up pieces of metal using machines. We can visualise it in our mind and it appears. It is a quicker and more efficient manner of producing anything than welding or bolting bits of metal together as you do on Earth.

The first thing we wish to bring to your attention, is that not all UFOs are flying saucer shape.

Depending on the group that is making one and depending on the use it is going to be put to, a UFO can be one of a number of shapes; saucer shaped, cigar shaped and a whole variety of variants.

It is, in a way, similar to the models of transport developed on Earth; small cars, large ones, buses of various types, trucks or lorries and so on.

There are very small craft designed to transport just one or two PLFs into physicality, up to huge craft, capable of acting rather in the manner of an aircraft carrier that you construct, housing many smaller craft and a large number of PLF.

Some of these ships can be of staggering size, but there are not many of these and are rarely seen, as they tend to stay in orbit, remote from planet Earth. You call them mother ships, just as you call the smaller craft scout craft. It is a fair description.

We insist on repeating that, whatever the shape and size of the UFO, it is, first and foremost in the astral realms, and only becomes physical when the decision is taken to bring it into physicality.

So, let us, while we are mentioning that subject, clear up the debate of the vast distances UFOs must travel, this being a reason that detractors of Ufology say that UFOs cannot exist. It would take too long to get from some distant star cluster to Earth, even at the speed of light.

This is where it starts to get almost comical. As we mentioned earlier, popular belief claims that aliens are physical beings and live close to one of a number of star systems, countless light years distance from Earth, and the Pleiades, Sirius and Zeta Reticuli have been mentioned.

So, the distance that those star systems are from Earth, and it is accepted fact that nothing can travel faster than the speed of light, therefore no alien would live long enough to get here.

That presents conclusive proof that aliens do not exist, even though there is an increasing number of photographs and films of UFOs seen in the sky and more and more people are seeing UFOs.

One wonders how one of these people who claim that UFOs do not exist would react if he saw one himself? Perhaps his mind would just refuse to accept the evidence of his eyes and he would convince himself that it was his imagination at work and, in reality, he saw a bird or a shooting star - or marsh gas!

But the truth is that UFOs don't really travel any distance at all.

The astral realms are all around us, so it is not a question of travelling, but of altering frequency in which case, when filmed, they are suddenly observed to blink into our reality and blink out when they no longer desire to be here.

Once in 3D reality, if they wish to travel from one place to another, they use a "jumping" technique that we have already described in a video but will describe again a bit later.

As you can imagine, the elements that go into the construction of a UFO, are not only very complicated from Earth humans point of view but, to a certain degree, different elements are used because, just like humans incarnate, different groups use different methods to construct similar objects.

For instance, in the case of an automobile, an engine might be powered by petrol (gasoline), diesel fuel or by electric current. If it were not for the governments of countries hiding the truth about other power sources, zero-point energy would also be available to power vehicles and other objects.

Now, we will not mention names, but there is one gentleman that noticed that the UFO he was studying was powered in a rather complicated manner using an element, 115, that is not really available on Earth.

It is not our place to point fingers, because we feel that the person concerned acted in faith according to where his investigations took him, but we will say that, as far as we know, his conclusions were not correct.

Any form of power source must be made of materials that exist in astral form first and then can be altered to appear in physicality.

The type of propulsion and movement, described by this person, in physicality could, in theory, be manufactured in physicality, but could not exist in astral form first.

So, we wish you to comprehend, that anything that exists in the astral world has to be made of pure astral material, and act first in astral form before the frequency being lowered so as to appear and operate in physicality.

Therefore, let us first say, that any flying craft manufactured by man incarnate - even if it is claimed to use technology back engineered from crashed UFOs, or to have been given by the Grey aliens, is using technology of a purely physical nature.

An astral power source has to have a spiritual base, because all that exists in non-physicality is of a spiritual nature.

We stress that we do not put any religious connotation on the word "spiritual". We refer to the fact that as all is one, a UFO must have elements that all life has.

For example, we have stressed over and over again that anything, animal, vegetable or mineral must have the non-physical elements before a physical version can be created.

So, just to take humans, there is the spiritual part that we talked about at great length; personality bundles, Higher Self, Imagination, ID, etc.

Thus, a UFO must have the same spiritual elements to it.

Something made on Earth, an aeroplane, a car, a TV, or whatever, is made in a physical form, even though each atom from which the item is constructed has an astral form.

But, if something is formed in the astral planes and then lowered in frequency so as to be able to operate in physicality, not only does each atom have to have an astral form, but the whole concept must also have an astral form.

By which we imply that it has to have a spiritual - non-physical - power source, just as a human or an animal has actually a spiritual power source that keeps the physical part going.

We have mentioned that an onion is an alive vegetable but, when peeled, the power source - the life force - cannot be found and yet was there to make the onion grow.

It is the same with a human or an animal. No matter into how many slices it might be cut, the power source cannot be found.

Therefore, for any true UFO, the power source is not visible. It does not seem to contain a power source. If dismantled into all its component parts, nothing would be found to give any indication of its power source, any more than we can see if we disrobe an onion or an animal or human.

That is one of the reasons why we can say with certainty, that the UFO that used element 115 and a mass of other components to make it fly, was not a true UFO.

If that particular craft existed, either a mistake as to its propulsion system was made or it was suggested by the Grey aliens to misguide humanity.

A true UFO is grown very much in the manner that all living things are grown and a true UFO is alive. It has to be because you are alive and all is one. Therefore, if you are alive, a UFO is alive.

Life can take many forms.

We mentioned, when talking about the various robots generally called Grey's, that we did not really understand how energy was sucked from the cosmos to keep the grey robot going and, we are afraid, we must say the same about the power source that fuels a true UFO.

Obviously, we have ideas and theories, but we must admit that we do not have conclusive proof and therefore we prefer to refrain from speculation.

The day we are sure, and if we feel that man incarnate could understand, we will inform you but, for the moment, we are not sure.

Let us take a look inside a UFO and see if there's any technology that we can understand, and possibly back engineer.

Now, once again, we need to separate fact from fiction.

It has been suggested that some elements have made their way through to the public domain.

For instance, integrated circuits have been mentioned, glass fiber optic tubes have been mentioned and a number of other things.

The claim is that they have been back engineered from downed spacecraft and have been released to the public.

But we have to say, once again, we can find no proof of this.

It is possible that the Grey's have manufactured craft with these elements in them, have force landed the craft and traded this technology with military groups so as to obtain whatever the Grey's want.

But a true UFO is actually grown in the astral worlds, which is why there are no nuts and bolts holding the outer shell together, and is actually closer to a living being, when seen in physical form, and actually has no keyboards, glass fiber cables, etc., any more than you have.

It is alive in the sense that it is first and foremost a non-physical object, and it is this non-physical aspect that creates it just as it does with you or any other living object.

These craft may well be designed to carry the alien robots and/or scout craft but doesn't need any robot to fly it.

If you imagine it to be alive, almost in the sense that you are alive, you do not need any robot to enable you to move about. Your non-physical aspects perform all this in the astral planes.

With a true UFO, the brain controlling it is what we referred to as an alien, which we discussed earlier.

The alien tells it what to do very much as your non-physical aspects do and, just as your body follows orders of your non-physical aspects, the UFO follows the order of the alien who always remains in the astral worlds.

As we have mentioned, the UFO is primarily in the astral realms and if a decision is taken to bring it into physicality, it is just lowered in frequency and we see it in our physical world.
But it remains under the control of the alien in the astral realms.

In a true UFO there are no seats and no one flies it other than the alien who remains in the astral realm.

So, as we said, there are no kitchens, no bathrooms, no dining halls, no bedrooms, no medical facilities, even in the largest motherships.
No one on board eats, sleeps, excretes or has need of medical treatment.

The passengers - robots - are purely astral in nature until the moment that a decision is taken to bring the UFO and any occupants into physicality, at which point the frequency of the ship and any occupants is lowered and it blinks into our (your) reality.

Now, let us make a slight detour and deal with the several ships that have been captured and are in military custody.
Generally speaking, a vast hoax has been placed on the public, and a number of saucer shaped craft have been manufactured by man and placed in various hangers. These are not craft that could fly.
They are often just "mock-ups" and are created in case anyone, military or civilian in authority, should demand to see a craft. He/she could be escorted to a hanger and shown the craft(s). Of course, they would be warned not to approach too closely because of radiation. In fact, some - indeed most - of these craft are just empty shells.

However, there are, from time to time, UFOs that crash and are recovered, usually by American military. These are usually Grey UFOs that are given as gifts in order to muddy the waters.
No true alien craft would crash. They have safeguards that would prevent any mechanical failure. In fact, "mechanical" is not the correct word, because they are actually astral appliances and the frequency has just been lowered to enter so-called physicality.
In the almost impossible event of something going wrong, the UFO would instantly return to its astral form, in which case, nothing can harm it.

We will also say that a true UFO, when seen in physicality in the skies, is not really in 3D reality.
Just as, when a person meditates and visits another dimension, his physical body remains on Earth and he enters one of his auras to visit another dimension.
Similarly, but conversely, the natural state for a UFO is in the astral realms.
UFOs, being alive, have auras just as all living things have, so if the alien decides to enter 3D reality, it changes the consciousness of the UFO to an aura that corresponds to 3D.

So, the original ship stays in the astral realms and the concentration on a 3D aura creates a copy in 3D.

This is not easy to understand but if you realise that a human can be meditating on Earth and can reach out with his consciousness to an auric dimension, in the case of a UFO, it is the same but in reverse.
The ship remains in auric form, but the alien projects the idea that he wishes the ship to enter 3D and a 3D version appears.

It has been noticed that some craft are clearly seen in the skies. These are the UFOs of Grey manufacture.

Genuine alien craft, if seen, are often observed to be slightly fuzzy looking. This is because the form created by alien consciousness and the degree of concentration by the alien controlling the ship, may not be 100%.
Therefore, the craft may be visible, but is not totally formed in our 3D.
As you can imagine, it is not easy for a personality bundle, that we term an alien, to concentrate totally on the 3D craft that he is concentrating on, and thus the image seen is not always totally formed.
It has also been noticed by some people that craft sometimes appear and disappear - blink in and out of 3D.
That occurs when the alien is not sufficiently concentrating on the task of visualising his craft in 3D. The alien's mind might be wandering, so to speak, and so the UFO is seen in 3D, then returns to astral form, blinks into 3D again and blinks back to astral form.

So, we hope that you can now understand that there are, basically, two types of UFOs. One is the true UFO which is created, one might even say born, in the astral realms and can sometimes visit us here on Earth, or go anywhere in the galaxy, and the second sort are those flying craft manufactured by what you refer to as the Grey's.

It is time to move on to look at the Grey population.
It is rather an unpleasant topic to discuss, but we need to bring this group to public awareness.
This will be the subject of the next chapter.

CHAPTER 12

GREY UFOs – AN OVERVIEW

In the last chapter we implied that there were two types of aliens and UFOs.
The genuine UFOs were created by the personality bundles and we said that the second, or false UFOs, are created by the Grey's.
So, this chapter will be devoted to telling you about the Grey's, as they are called.

Like all subjects, this is a complicated one, and the problem is always to know where to start, and so if we jump around somewhat we hope you will forgive us.
Perhaps we should start by describing, once again, the lower fourth dimension which, as we have already stated in other works, is where the dark, demonic forces live.

Now, we have already mentioned that life contains two sorts of forces, both of which are necessary to keep life in balance; the forces for construction and the forces for destruction.
We are not interested in those beings at this moment because they do not concern the subject of this book.
However, as we have often stated, all dimensions are multitasking, and so the fourth dimension is divided into two parts - the higher fourth, as it is called, is where the positive elements of existence live (in part at least), whereas the lower fourth is where the opposite to positivity exists. Negativity.
Among these negative elements are what are referred to as demons.

Demons are, in a way, similar to angels but, obviously, act in a completely opposite way to angels.
Angels are totally concentrated on doing good for all life whereas demons are concentrating all their energies on doing harm.

It may be questioned as to why they exist, but all life must be kept in balance, so it is necessary to have an equilibrium between positivity and negativity - yin and yang.
We have explained this principle in detail in other works.

Now, demons are very similar to humans, in that they have personality bundles and a form of Higher Self, Imagination and ID, etc. But they are not programmed to have any aspect of them appear in physicality. They always remain in etheric and/or astral realms.

We repeat, whatever type of demon they might be, and there are several types, the common denominator is that they are all negative.
They have no conception of positivity at all. This is not hate. It is just the way that they were created by the Archangels that created all life and are an essential part of the balance of life.

Life is very complicated and, without going into a long discussion of the rights and wrongs of angels and demons, which we have already described in other works, we ask you to accept that demons exist and always remain in non-physicality.

However, we have also mentioned Archons, and although Archons are a completely different species to demons, the aims and objectives are much the same and so it is not unknown for Archons to work with demons to influence man in negative ways.

But that is a different topic. This book is about how alien life interacts with man incarnate, so we will not go any further in a discussion that would take us outside of the concepts of this book.

Therefore, we wish to make it clear to you that a demon, being created by the God force, is alive and thus has eight auras and eight personality bundles and all the other attributes that all life has.
The one missing element is the fact that demons have never been programmed to have an Earthly incarnation, so all eight versions of any demon remain in non-physicality.

But like many life forms, demons have curiosity and so some of them feel the desire to interact with man incarnate.
Thus, like the more positive personality bundles we have mentioned above, the idea of creating UFOs and robot life forms occurred to them.

We mentioned that we would have to jump around somewhat in this chapter so we break off to dispel the concept of "fallen angels".
It has been written in various religious books, a story about Satan having been an angel who, somehow, took the wrong route and was cast from heaven with a number of fallen angels but we hope that you can see from the explanation we have given you, that this is not true at all.
Quite why such a story was invented is not our concern, but we will state that Satan, the devil, old Nick or whatever title he is given, does not exist - only as a thought form to scare people into following a religion.
But demons do exist.
They are not fallen angels, but life forces created to help keep life in balance.
We will also say that it is almost impossible for the average person to fall under the influence of a demon.

Demons remain in areas remote from man.
The concept of being possessed was invented by priests, who created religions and the motive behind it was, and is, to entrap people into a religion.
The only people who are able to have any interaction with negative forces are magicians, who study the black arts for many years before opening the door between physicality and the lower fourth dimension.
Even in that case, the only beings a black magician could contact would be a Djinn - a low powered demon.

The higher-powered demons remain remote from all but the most advanced magicians, who have devoted virtually their whole life to this study and also have the means to congregate in secret.

Ordinary people do not have the time or the financial and political force to create complicated ceremonies in total camera (secret).

If the average person was to hold regular black magic ceremonies in a normal house, the neighbours would soon notice that something bizarre was going on.

Therefore, there are the relatively few psychopaths, immensely rich and influential, but that hope to get ever more power, and have huge private domains, remote from public gaze, with private means of transport and that have set up a network of ways and means of procuring what they need to fulfill the requirements of a black mass that operates totally outside of public awareness.

Now, not all these people are capable of summoning a demon, but some are capable of producing and concentrating etheric material that a demon can attach itself to for a while. But, as demons are negative, to summon a demon requires a large degree of negativity. We will not go into details, but we will say that these misguided souls who practice black magic and who commit horrendous crimes in their practices, are deceived.

A demon, being negative, can only create negativity and so the practitioners receive nothing as a reward for the negativity they create.

Further, once their lives are over and they return to the heavenly spheres and have to pay for their crimes, they spend long years in hell before they expunge their sins.

So, to practise black magic, one is deceived twice.

First by the false and broken promises made by the demons and second by the degree of remorse they must go through because of the sins they committed.

We hope that we have made it plain to all that, by the Law of Mutual Attraction, if one gets involved in negativity - evil - one will reap evil and suffering.

Having broached that very unpleasant topic, let us return to the discussion of demons and UFOs, etc.

We mentioned, in discussing what we call real UFOs, that the spaceships are grown in the astral realms and are alive, having all the attributes of any living thing - including a soul (a God aspect).

It may require a stretch of the imagination to think of a flying saucer as being alive and of having a soul, but it is so.

The Archangels who are charged by God to create life, are also given the responsibility for deciding what may have a soul and what may not.

Demons have souls, being a necessary aspect of life, but the Archangels do not want the evil powers to spread unbridled, so any creation by a demon is not permitted a soul and thus would not be alive.

We have mentioned this in relation to hybrids. Any hybrid, a mixture of human and demon, would not be permitted to have a soul and so could not actually live very long.

Therefore, any UFO created by demons could not be grown in astral form. There would be no spiritual aspect to it.

So, long ago, little PLFs were created in physicality and were instructed to create a few UFOs.

We might well ask how this was done, because if a lower fourth UFO is examined, it is found to contain a number of elements that, even today, do not exist in physicality, or if they do they are recent inventions: computers, keyboards, fiber optic cables and all sorts of advanced things.

These are recent inventions.

Indeed, much of what exists in a "not real UFO" still doesn't exist to this day in our world.

Let us break off again for a moment and decide what to call these demonic designed UFOs.

Let us just call them Grey UFOs. We hope you understand that when we mention Grey UFOs, we are referring to the ones created by creatures from the lower fourth dimensions.

But we wish you also to realise that life has come and gone many times over vast periods of time and so we can be sure that some very advanced scientists of those days were influenced by demonic forces to construct the first Grey UFOs, based on the technology that was available on Earth at that time.

So, the first Grey UFOs were man-made a long time ago, using the technologies that had already been created by advanced man in a now long dead civilisation. No doubt the first robots were also created by man.

So, the difference between real UFOs and Grey UFOs is this.

A real UFO is a living object, just like any other living object and is born in the astral realms, just like any other living creature is.

A Grey UFO is man made - or was - and is a robotic machine like a car, an aeroplane, or anything else man-made and thus is not alive.

It is perhaps worth repeating this to make it perfectly clear.

A real UFO is a living object - although the PLF that the personality bundle would create in the astral realms may or may not be alive in the sense of having a soul.

A demon is alive.

Human life on planet Earth goes back a long way and has developed and been eliminated by catastrophes many times.

Some of these races were very advanced indeed compared to modern man.

You may remember us saying to you, that life has spent a great deal of time in negativity and is only now moving into positivity.

So, it was easy for the demonic spirits, at that time, to take control of scientists who were very negative, and influence them to create Grey UFOs and Grey PLF.

We hope you now have a clear picture of the difference between a true UFO and a Grey UFO.

Now, even though those scientists of that time were very advanced, sufficiently advanced as to be able to design and construct the first UFOs, compared to true aliens, they were still fairly primitive.

As they constructed the first Grey UFOs in physicality, naturally they used the technology that was available to them at that time.
Thus, as they had invented computers, keyboards and fiber optics, they incorporated them into the Grey UFOs. They also constructed PLFs and programmed them to operate the ships.

Assuming that what we have said about the Greys to be correct and, naturally, we are sure of our facts, or we would not state them, the Greys had UFOs a long time ago.

We will repeat, demons do not have the ability to move into physicality, so any UFOs or PLFs have to be created on Earth from Earth material.
That does not mean that everything would be as primitive as technology is on Earth today.
The technology used dates back many years, when a very advanced human species was incarnate, that was eventually wiped out by a global catastrophe and life had to begin again.

But the technology remains and is hidden away from public gaze.

Now, if we go back to the Roswell incident of 1947, it is our understanding that the Grey's wanted to give us the gift of one or more UFOs and PLFs but, through an error, one UFO crashed and was destroyed along with the PLF.
Then, of course, a further error was committed by allowing the public to be informed that alien life was here on Earth.
As we mentioned earlier, this error was immediately rectified and a UFO was presented to the public as a balloon. The amazing thing is that most people accepted this idiotic story without question.
To make sure that the truth did not spread, many people had their lives threatened and some murders were committed.
Even these stupid acts did not arouse suspicion among the population.
One would have thought, that to reveal to the public photographs and reportages of a balloon, would hardly have warranted such massive attempts to cover up information about the balloon that had already been released to the public, but the majority of people accepted the balloon story and many, even today, are still asking the question, 'Do UFOs exist? And many are still answering, 'No'.

The fact that Grey UFOs and PLFs are frequently seen and filmed in the skies, connected to what we have said about these objects being created and repaired here on Earth, opens the door to a number of supplementary questions.

1. Where are they manufactured and repaired?
2. Where are the UFOs and PLFs stored when not in use?
3. Why did demons want UFOs to be able to explore so-called physicality?
4. What is the truth about abductions, mutilations, etc.

We will answer questions 1 and 2 here in this chapter.
The answers to many other aspects of Grey intervention will be discussed in other chapters.

Now, every time there was a catastrophe and all, or most, human and animal life eliminated, the Grey's withdrew all their craft and PLFs that they had that were fit to fly and took them elsewhere; the moon, Mars, etc., until life settled down again on Earth, at which point they returned.

You may have noticed in various paintings from all over the world, tiny UFOs sometimes depicted in a not-too-obvious part of the paintings.

The reason is that, in the past, it was quite a common sight to see UFOs in the sky or even on land.

But, people were very superstitious and, usually, badly educated.
So, these artists might well have seen Grey visitors, but had no idea of who they were or what they wanted.
Even cave paintings, made many years ago, depict them, but both the UFOs and the PLFs are drawn in much the same fashion as these cavemen painted humans and animals. They raised no more curiosity to these early humans than seeing other humans or animals did. They were just a fact of life and were accepted as part of everyday life.

Later, when religions got a stranglehold on humanity, it was thought that the Grey population were probably Gods or angels or visitors from heaven or hell, so might well have been depicted in a painting, but it was deemed unwise to question God's creation, so it was considered acceptable to include them in a religious painting, but it was better not to question God's creation.

Before we answer questions 1 and 2, let us jump forward to the moment when a president and the leader of a Christian church and various other people had been contacted by the Tall Whites - or Nordics - as they are sometimes called.
We have already explained that these people live on Earth and their craft are manufactured on Earth by them.

This group explained to the president and his associates, that to use thermonuclear devices was not the way to move forward and offered, if these terrible weapons would be disposed of, to help humanity to progress towards world peace.

They also said that a negative group would follow their visit and this group would be very harmful to man. They were referring to the Grey's.

The offer of the Tall Whites was refused and, a short while afterwards, the second group visited the same people who were present at the meeting with the Tall Whites and offered to supply advanced technology in exchange for certain favours.

This second group were the Grey's.

Their offer was immediately accepted.

Now, the Grey's had already a number of bases they used in which to manufacture, repair and store their craft and PLFs, usually in remote areas of the world, but asked for deep underground bases to be constructed in which they could conduct their affairs in secret.

These bases are sometimes referred to as D.U.M.Bs (deep underground military bases). It is an apt term because the military must have been pretty dumb to accept any offer from demons!

However, such is the nature of military people, that any promise of advanced weapons of destruction appeals to their primitive instincts.

So, we have to this day the original hideaways that the Grey's have been using for long ages and, in addition, D.U.M.Bs in which they can operate in peace.

On top of which, the Grey's have been given total protection from investigation by the public and any attempt to reveal the Grey presence is hushed up by any and all means.

The one question that we will not answer is the power sources that are used to enable these Grey UFOs to fly.

In the case of true UFOs, we had to admit that we did not know what the technology used was that enable them to navigate in 3D physicality.

In the case of the Grey's, apart from saying that it is anti-gravity, the technology - given, don't forget by an advanced group of humans long ago - is so advanced compared to anything available on Earth now, that we would find it almost impossible to describe and you would not understand.

We wish to say before we end this chapter that the Greys, in an attempt to keep a semblance of respecting their part of the bargain - protection by the military in exchange for freedom to do whatever they want here on Earth - have given the military a number of UFOs as gifts.

But, much to the disappointment of the military, these Grey UFOs have proved impossible to fly by humans.

The excuse given by the Grey's is that humans today do not have the skill to fly Grey craft because the PLFs that pilot them have such advanced spiritual skills that they become one with the craft.

However, if we consider that a PLF has an IQ of about 80, this would not hold water.

In fact, the Greys create special UFO, incapable of flight, tow them to a spot and then drop them to ground and tell the military to go and pick up the gift.

The fact that, it would appear, the military spend a fortune back engineering something that could never create anti-gravity, gives some indication of the intelligence of high ranking military people.

It should be obvious that, when dealing with demons, they do all that is in their power to create unhappiness, and giving false gifts is just one of their ploys.
But the military mind is special!

We will end this chapter here and move on, although we are sure that there is still a lot more we could say about this demonic force.

CHAPTER 13

THE ABDUCTION EXPERIENCE

In this chapter, we will discuss the phenomenon known as 'alien abductions' and describe what really happens as far as we can because, like much to do with the subject of aliens, it is a multi-layered subject and not a "one answer fits all" event.

We can, however, break the subject down into two basic types of events.

1. A person might be outside of his/her house, either during the day or the night and is obliged to go into a spaceship. By outside of the house we mean remote from the house.

2. A person might be fast asleep in bed, either on their own or with someone else and they are suddenly aware of PLFs in the room who oblige them to go to a spaceship, often passing through solid walls.

In either case, there are usually very unpleasant medical type examinations that take place, some extremely painful, some not.

We feel that it will be easier to understand what is going on from the moment that the person is inside the UFO, try to explain exactly what is happening and then go back to the moment of the actual abduction later.

So, we will start from the moment that the person is inside the craft and follow the procedure.
Our aim is to help you understand exactly what an abduction is that some people now call an 'experience' and the person to whom it is happening an 'experiencer'.

The first thing that we need to point out is that what the abducted person notices is that sometimes they have the impression that they are in a circular craft and sometimes they feel that they are in a base of some kind, a physical building.

Also, they might notice a few PLFs around them and, further away, human looking doctors in lab coats, soldiers (sometimes) and various creatures - Mantis and Reptilians. So, in some cases there are a variety of entities observing what is going on, some human and some obviously not.

The actual abduction event can vary from one person - male or female - on their own, up to a large number of abducted people, who may be sitting in a classroom looking at TV type screens.
If the person is alone, they often find themselves naked and lying on a stainless steel table, unable to move, and a variety of medical examination instruments appear and are manipulated by the PLFs.

Even if there are 3 or 4 people in a similar situation, there are always the required number of tables and the required number of medical instruments.

And, we should add, the required number of 'doctors' or 'technicians', if we may thus term them, to cover any situation, almost as if the abductions had been pre-programmed and the required number of operatives brought in.

So, we need, perhaps, to ask a few questions before we can hope to get any intelligent answers as to what abductions are.

Before we delve into those questions, may we explain how we, the Great White Brotherhood, manage to observe any abductions and learn what people claim is happening to them?

We live, as you should be aware by now, in the astral realms.

But those realms always have a connection to what is referred to as 3-D physicality because, as we have explained many times and at great length, what you refer to as physicality is, in fact, just in or on one of the dimensions - the 6th dimension - and as we have the ability to move through the dimensions easily, we can, from the place where we normally reside, move our frequency to be in synchronicity with the 6th dimension and thus can observe directly what is going on as someone is abducted and also to examine the events taking place during the abduction experience.

We also have the ability to select a frequency almost identical to the frequency that the abduction events are taking place on but just slightly altered - phase shifted, if you wish - to enable us to remain invisible to all in 3D physicality but close enough that we can follow what is happening.

Next, we can bring the Akashic Record to our aid.

We have to explain that every event, anywhere connected to planet Earth and throughout all time, for all people, are recorded in the Akashic Record - the living library - so we can enter that realm and watch abductions, past and present, exactly as they happened.

We can observe an abduction as a film or we can slow it down, speed it up and even link, psychically, with the people taking part and study the event from their point of view, and/or from the point of view of any living creature connected to the event.

We will add that machines are not directly connected to the Akashic Record.

Therefore, we can look through the eyes of a human and look at a PLF but we could not observe the human through the eyes of the PLF, as that creature is not alive. It is just a machine, a robot.

Finally, we can use the Akashic Record in another fashion and look at all the films and videos created, some of them on celluloid film and some electronically and stored as videos available to anyone who has a computer and an internet connection. Although the actual film or video is not directly stored in the Akashic Record, not being alive, we can observe it through the eyes and memories of those who made the films or videos, so it comes to the same thing.

Thus, we hope you can appreciate from what we have just said about that, if we interest ourselves in alien abductions, there is not much about the events that escapes our attention.

Thus, individually and collectively, we are able to analyse the evidence before us and are able to draw intelligent conclusions.

We may work individually on any project that interests us but may also link, telepathically, to any other member of the Great White Brotherhood studying the same phenomenon and instantly know all the intelligence that they have garnered on a subject as an instant block of knowledge and, inversely, they can download any information that the first individual has.

This happens instantly and so, in a very short space of time, we are able to share any knowledge and thus combine our experiences, which enables us to have a vast amount of intelligence on any subject, a combined view of all Great White Brotherhood members that wish to share their knowledge on any subject.

In the case of alien abductions, this is exactly what we have done and so what we will explain on the subject is our collective view of what has been going on over a vast period of time and from all over the world, including anything that may be from other dimensions but relevant to the alien abduction scenario.

The first thing we wish to say is that abductions - or any other negative act - is never carried out by the group of "true" aliens, the personality bundles that we described earlier.

The only acts that the positive aliens are responsible for are when atomic missile silos or bunkers are interfered with.

The positive or true aliens heartily disapprove of war in general and nuclear war in particular and so they demonstrate to the military of various countries, from time to time, that they will not tolerate the use of such weapons.

This they do by demonstrating their ability to contact the arming and firing mechanisms of any nuclear based weapons, to give fair warning to anyone stupid enough to try to start a nuclear war, that this will not be allowed to happen.

We hope that the military and governmental authorities of the world have learnt this lesson by now and, although they still pose as if they are capable of nuclear aggression, in fact, know perfectly well that this will never be allowed to happen.

So, we know that all the abductions, mutilations and so on are either conducted by the Greys or certain factions of military that works to aid the Greys or to scare people to be afraid of aliens,

Most people do not know that there are two types of aliens - peaceful ones and harmful ones.

So, abductions and mutilations are conducted to paint a picture that all aliens are evil.

Now, abductions can take many forms but we wish to bring to your attention a few interesting points that raises questions as to what exactly is happening and in what dimension events might be occurring.

Let us also say that many abductees or experiencers return from an event with little or no memory that they were abducted.
It is only when they are addressed during hypnotic sessions that memories return and they relive the horrifying events of one or more abductions.

We should also mention that there are some people who create abductions entirely fictitiously - they never, in fact, happened.
There are a few reasons why people may do this and we touched on this topic earlier.
Everyone likes to feel special and the alien agenda is the latest one that people pick on to use in their pursuit of feeling special.

There are people who are mentally or emotionally weak and are quite often pushed onto the edge of society. Thus, they have no ability to feel that their existence is justified because all they have to show for their lives is a number of failed relationships and the number of visits to psychiatric establishments.
But, if they can claim to have something esoteric happened to them, who can deny that it is not true?
So, some people start to channel angelic beings, St. Michael, Jesus, Mary, God, etc.
And the surprising thing is that others believe them and so the unwell person is encouraged to go on and on using social media to create groups to whom these messages are given.
The fact that others accept this information as real is, perhaps, a sign of just how sad, lost and confused so many people are and to be told that these angelic beings are caring for them, are aware of and dealing with worldly affairs to create a paradise on Earth, so would accept unquestioningly these messages.

We should, in fairness, say that the same criticism could apply to us - the Great White Brotherhood - because for a number of years now we have been telling you that we are moving from darkness into light.
However, although we can present little or no proof that we are not just a group of mentally ill people creating fantasy, we leave you to judge if we are rational, sane beings and what we tell you is fact, not fiction, no matter how bizarre some of it sounds.

These somewhat unwell people, if they don't create channelled messages from saints, might go down the road of abductions.
After all, internet and conferences are full of people recounting similar stories of having been abducted, sperm and ova taken and hybrid children produced, etc.

Books may be written describing multiple abductions dating back to childhood, any number of gory details concerning operations conducted and on and on.

Then, once the book published, the UFO conference circuit can be approached and, pretty soon, the person can earn a living giving talks describing abductions, hybrid children, trips to various planets in UFOs, etc.

All fictitious, but that no one questions.

Now, please understand that we described above the many unbalanced people who create a Walter Mitty world in which to live.

Everyone has the right to live in whatever reality they create but to distract other people to believe them is not helpful.

So, please do not think that we are saying that all people who have abductions are mentally ill. We are not.

But there is a point that is somewhat baffling.

This is the subject of needing to use "the bathroom", as it is called when referring to need to pass urine or excreta.

Anyone who is woken up in the middle of the night and told to follow someone from the bedroom for some reason, would quite often say that they need to visit the bathroom first.

But, in the case of abductees suddenly lifted from their beds in the middle of the night, our investigations have never revealed anyone requesting to visit the bathroom before moving out of the house.

Similarly, those who are abducted from the exterior of the house, perhaps in a car, and are stripped naked, laid on a cold stainless steel table, in the UFO that they often mentioned as being cold has, to our knowledge, never mentioned requesting to use the bathroom in the UFO.

Those who have ever been to a meeting or conference on Earth where there might be a hundred people will know that, pretty soon, there will be people heading for the toilets. This never seems to happen in multiple UFO abductions.

We have watched people describe witnessing a number of children, abducted and being taught in spaceships.

Anyone who has worked in schools with young children will know that regular visits to the bathroom occur.

But not with abducted children.

As the last thing, women of childbearing age, if frequently abducted, would, one imagines, be having their monthly period from time to time but it is rare that any woman complains of having been abducted, stripped naked at this delicate time of the month and left lying naked on the table.

One would have thought that the memory of such an unpleasant event would have remained uppermost in her mind, but no. It is seldom ever mentioned.

So, what is going on here?

People being abducted in vast numbers worldwide but never needing to use the bathroom?
Women of childbearing age never complaining of being abducted during the menstrual cycle period.

Would you agree that there is something bizarre occurring?

Then, of course, we have the situation of people being taken for several days out into space and shown various things.
Not only is there never mention of needing to visit "the bathroom" but never any desire to eat.
If they are taken on a conducted tour of the ship, we have never heard of anyone mentioning the toilet area, the kitchens, the dining areas, bedrooms or any of the things that we would need.
Never any description of any food given.

Of course, now that we have mentioned this, perhaps abductees will start to mention bathrooms and kitchens but, up till now, of all the cases we have studied worldwide, these places have never been mentioned.
Equally, during the question and answer sessions at the end of a lecture, these questions have seldom or never been raised.

Would you agree that there is something not totally "Earth like" in all this?

We, when incarnate, remember having the desire to eat fairly frequently and the need to visit the bathroom at regular intervals - but not once we are in the Astral Realms, once our incarnations terminated, and neither do people inside spaceships, or hangers, apparently.
Perhaps there is a connection here worth considering?

We wish you to know that we have studied thousands of cases, not only from America but from all over the world, cases presented by people of all ages, skin colour, education and so on and never from conscious memory, nor from hypnotic regression, has anyone any memory of eating or using toilets during abductions.
It is also interesting that seldom or never, during hypnotic regression sessions, has the person conducting the regression ever asked these questions.

From our point of view, if we were involved with abductees, these are among the first questions to which we would seek answers, to try to verify in what plane of reality all this was occurring: 3D reality or in astral (etheric) form.

One last point on this subject. People claim to have seen hybrid children, some quite human looking.
Do these hybrids need to eat and eliminate if they really have human looking bodies?
Once again, if there are no kitchens for food preparation and no toilets to take care of the other end of the digestive process, are true beings being described?

Once again, we get no answer from the people being abducted.

So, can we step back from all this and find out really what the abduction scenario is all about?

Fortunately, thanks to the Akashic Records, where the truth about the actual events are stored, we can see what abductions are about.
We had better just say, before we continue, in the case of an abduction, two versions are stored in the Akashic Record. The first is what the abductee experienced and the second is just a recording of what actually happened.

If we may give a simple example. If we look at a scene from a movie, we see the result as presented on the silver screen.
But if we see a documentary of how that scene was constructed, we have the script writers who work with the producers and director of the film who, in turn, work with a host of other people; set designers, creators of clothing, sound and light engineers, makeup artists and the actors and, eventually, a scene is recorded and projected in a cinema.
So, we can see that, behind the scene, as we might watch it in a cinema, is another set of events that eventually create the final scene.

Therefore, we can have recorded, two versions of a scene:
1. The version you watch on the screen, and
2. A description of what really happened.

In the case of abductions, we have two events similar to what we have described above:
1. We have the event as described by an abductee, and
2. A version of what really occurred that enabled the abduction scenario to happen.

Now, this is where we need to tread carefully, because we do not wish to step on people's toes, so to speak, but at the same time we have the obligation to tell the truth about abduction events.

We have already said that of the two types of aliens, all abductions are created by the demonic ones, and/or the military, who have been given, by the demonic Greys, the knowledge of how to abduct people.

The modus operandi of demons is negativity. They exist to create negativity - fear.
So, we can be sure that any act by negative aliens will be negative - unpleasant.

Perhaps, before we take the plunge to describe the actions of the Grey group of aliens, we could return for a moment to the true aliens who are, by and large, positive, helpful.

We said that the only act that the good aliens would do was to prevent mankind from destroying the Earth by nuclear weapons and this is, by and large, true.

However, they are constantly monitoring situations on Earth and, although they generally do not interfere with man, can and do if they feel the occasion merits it.

We will not go into details except to say that the true, positive aliens, are constantly monitoring events on many levels; not only here on Earth but throughout the galaxy and trying to correct actions by others that would cause great harm.

But let us return to the abduction scenario.

We deliberately, and at some length, mentioned about bathrooms and kitchens and tried to get you to question what was happening, because we wanted you to try to accept that there was something not entirely physical about an abduction.

We will ignore the people who have emotional problems and invent abductions, which is so easy to imagine from the mass of abduction stories that are on internet or described in the many books written by abductees or experiencers. These deluded people might or might not finish by believing what they have imagined but the fact remains, did they get abducted or did they not?

We leave them to resolve those issues themselves.

So, let us move on to examine what really happens to genuine abductees.

We have to say that none of it is physical, much that what is experienced seems perfectly real.

The bathroom story we recounted should be enough to indicate to all reasonable people that abductions cannot be physical because, if there are no toilets facilities on board a spacecraft - or kitchens for that matter - the floors of the spacecraft would soon be awash in urine.

Who has ever seen aliens swabbing urine with mops and buckets in UFOs? No one!

Who has ever seen washing water on a spacecraft?

There is never anything on a UFO related to bodily functions, either in terms of food, cleanliness or toilets.

It just doesn't exist.

Has anyone who spent, perhaps, a week on a spaceship, returned starving hungry and running for the nearest toilet?

It doesn't happen!

They leave the UFO at the same weight as when they entered it a week previously.

So, we must say that spacecraft are real and, in the case of the Grey ones, manufactured on Earth in secret hideouts.

PLFs are real physical entities, robots, manufactured also on Earth.

These UFOs and even, sometimes, the little PLFs remain in our reality.

The Grey demonic forces always remain in the astral realms but are able to communicate with certain military people either through telepathy or using some PLFs that have been fitted with voice boxes.

Therefore, there is a large element of the UFO phenomenon that is entirely physical and some, at least, of what is reported about underground bases by so-called whistleblowers is accurate.

But the abduction phenomenon is not entirely physical.
Once again this is going to be difficult to explain and even more difficult to accept by people who have been abducted and, either by memory or by hypnotic recall, are totally convinced that what they experienced was real.
In a way it was real. Real but not physical.

Let us take the case of someone driving along a country road and is taken.
You will notice that it is rare, indeed, for any person or family to be abducted from a car in a busy thoroughfare.

Usually what occurs is that the driver is instructed to turn off a busy interstate or motorway, down a side road and out into a deserted area where the car would not be disturbed.
After all, if a car suddenly stopped on a busy Interstate highway, it would not be long before it attracted the attention of a passing patrol car and the police would notice that either the occupants were missing or were in a deep trance.
Either way, action would be taken against the wishes of the abductors.

Thus, the car is directed to a remote area.
From there the abduction takes place and the people finally directed back to their car.

There are reports of cars being lifted, occupants and all, into the air and taken inside the spacecraft.
Now, what the recordings stored in the Akashic Record actually indicate is that, using a mind control technique, the people are put in a trance and it is their etheric double, including the etheric (created) image of the car if necessary, that is taken from the people and placed inside a created version of the spaceship.

This obviously needs to be explained carefully.

All living creatures - including humans - are multidimensional beings.
Therefore, you should know by now if you have followed our teachings, that you have, just next to your physical body, a copy that is called the etheric double.
This etheric double is actually many layered.
When people do astral projection, they enter the etheric double and wander about in an alternative reality.

Now, the aliens - the negative ones - are able to create a form of etheric double of their craft, or even bases in which the PLF are stored, and within these created areas are able to transport the etheric double of the abductees.

The physical bodies, once their consciousness is placed associated with the etheric double, just sleeps or is in a trance.

So, the abductee, with his consciousness now placed within his etheric double, finds himself in the etheric double of whatever is required, spaceship or base somewhere.

Therefore, all the experiments conducted on their body is actually occurring in the etheric double, that seems real to the abductee, just as a person who does astral projection feels it is real.

It is real, but not physical.

Now, we will also say that it is possible to abduct a person physically but it is rarely done because, as we mentioned, a physical person has "calls of nature" and UFOs are not equipped for dealing with bodily fluids.

So, it is more convenient to abduct the etheric double of a person, from which point they can access the mind of the sleeping person and thus connect with all the personal knowledge that the abducted person has.

The object, as we have often mentioned, is to find out, not only about human emotions, but in the hopes, also, of discovering the soul (the God spirit).

Thus, the aliens hope that if they can create souls and if they know all about people's personalities, they can create hybrids, not only with souls but with all the attributes of men and women.

The babies shown to ladies are etheric in nature - non-physical.

The people who have breastfed babies without being able to produce milk in physicality can do so in the etheric realms, because the etheric realm is also one of imagination and thus, if the lady imagines she is breastfeeding a child, the milk flows.

But it is not physical milk. It is imaginary milk feeding an imaginary baby.

So, assuming you believe what we are telling you, you can see that, once one is in the etheric world - which is a carbon copy of the real Earth - it is simple to pass through solid walls or through the roof of the house because, although to the person involved it seems just as real and solid as our (your) normal Earth, it is all actually non-physical. A solid looking wall or window is a form of imaginary construct in the etheric realm.

Thus, the physical body of the person remains in bed while the etheric double is in a parallel version of Earth but in this etheric or astral form. It is a form of astral projection, except that it is being provoked either by the demonic entities or by a section of the military who work with - and sometimes in competition with - the Greys.

In either case, all that happens is being done in the etheric realms.

As we mentioned, all this seems just as real as it would do if the physical body was being abducted.

Although we have already mentioned this, we will repeat, it occasionally occurs that the physical person is abducted but it is rare because, as we mentioned, the physical body has the need to eat and to eliminate, whereas the etheric body does not, so it is easier to abduct people etherically.

The etheric body is alive, while the physical body is alive, and so has access to all the emotions, thoughts and knowledge that the physical person has.

There are still a number of questions that remain to be answered.

1. Why are people always undressed during an abduction?
The answer is that the concept of entering a hospital, if one requires an operation, is known to most people and so it is accepted that a change of garb is required if any medical procedure is going to be performed.
The patient enters a hospital, is required to remove his street clothes and put on the sterile clothing provided by the hospital.
The patient is then placed on a bed.
As, during abductions, we are working in an imaginary world - the etheric - the mind of the abductee automatically switches on to what they think should happen in an operation and so the person feels the desire to remove his/her street clothes or night apparel.
However, no hospital garb is provided so the person feels naked.

Then, in a real hospital, the person is placed in a bed.
So, in the etheric realm a similar event occurs except that, instead of it being a fairly comfortable hospital bed, the concept of a stainless steel table is projected by the Greys into the mind of the abducted person.

Have you ever questioned why abducted people, stark naked, do not feel embarrassed when there are a number of abducted humans together, all totally naked?
After all, humans might be comfortable appearing naked in front of their wives or husbands but would be very embarrassed at being naked in close proximity to total strangers.
But abducted people never seem to mention this.
The reason is that it is because, in the etheric realm, this type of emotion has no relevance, so no one feels embarrassed.

2. Why is it that people sometimes return from an abduction with their clothes on the wrong way round or wearing someone else's clothes?
The answer to this is that it doesn't. The person remains in bed or in a vehicle or whatever, and his/her etheric double is taken. The physical body is not tampered with. Now, we will admit that on rare occasions a person is physically taken, in which case the person might be redressed with something amiss but, if taken etherically, the physical clothing would not be tampered with.

So, we have given a fairly in-depth view of what happens during an abduction.

Obviously, with all these types of events we could say much more but we would finish up with ridiculously large volumes that no one would read. Thus, we give an overview and hope that, from the information provided, you can extrapolate yourself to try to answer any other questions that might occur to you.

If you bear in mind that, usually, an abduction is happening in the etheric realms, you should be able to answer any questions that would seem to be impossible in physicality.

CHAPTER 14

ANIMAL MUTILATIONS

We think that you will agree that, so far in this book, we have covered a number of topics, many of which will be new to you and, perhaps, difficult to comprehend.
This is perfectly understandable because, as we have previously explained, no new information can be assimilated, accepted, unless a sort of pigeonhole is created in the mind in which to store the information.

Thus, it is inevitable that many of you will reject what we have told you in this unusual description of aliens and abductions.
The fact that a subject cannot be accepted does not mean that it is not true, it just means that you have no means of accepting the information.

If you do not have a pigeon hole created in the mind in which to store information, you have to reject that information until such times as a pigeon hole is formed, and then you have the possibility, at least, to consider, intelligently, the information presented and weigh the pros and cons in your own mind.

The mind likes, always, to stay on safe ground, which is why, in modern times, the subject of UFOs and aliens were made fun of - aided and abetted by governments and military who wanted this subject to remain secret.

When UFOs started to appear in concrete form in the 1940's - particularly once atomic weapons were invented - nobody wanted to accept that this frightening possibility was reality and so the coverup started. The military and the governments found it as difficult to accept UFOs and aliens as real as the average person of that time would have.
Now, rejection of a reality can take a number of forms.
As we have just mentioned, until one has a pigeon hole formed, rejection has to take place, but even if and when the pigeon hole is formed, if the subject is considered frightening - and at that time people (beings) appearing from out of the sky in strange looking craft, with strange looking lifeforms on the some of them, was reason to be very frightened.

So, to create an atmosphere of denial, it was decided to mock the UFO phenomenon and anyone who thought that UFOs were real was considered deranged.
At the same time, dreadful action was taken against anyone claiming to have seen or have knowledge of a UFO.

However, times are gradually changing and most people are aware today that UFOs exist.

What is not known, of course, is who they are and where they come from, which is why we are presenting this book to you.

There would be no point in us just repeating that they come from some distant star cluster when we know perfectly well who and what they are and where they come from.

So, we present the truth as we know it to be, and we must say that a small section of military intelligence also knows and leave it to you to accept or reject this information.

So now let us turn to another topic of the UFO phenomenon, once again very difficult to discuss, which is animal and human mutilations.

We are sure that most of you are aware of this horrific act but, for the few who do not know, a variety of animals; horses, cows, sheep and even wild animals are discovered dreadfully cut about, drained completely of blood. We have to say that, occasionally, even humans are found similarly mutilated.
To make matters worse, there is some evidence that these mutilations are carried out while the poor creatures, or humans, are alive and conscious.
If these acts are carried out, acts of unspeakable cruelty, we can be sure that the true aliens would not be involved.
Nor would any being from the higher astral realms.

So, we must assume that these vivisections are either being carried out by humans and/or the demonic aliens - the same ones that perform the abductions that we mentioned in the previous chapter.

So, if we employ the same investigation techniques that we used to discover the truth about abductions, we can find the truth about vivisections, known as animal mutilations.

We have to admit that many of them are carried out by Earth humans.

Trainee or student doctors or biologists consider it perfectly normal to take live frogs and cut them up to study the nervous systems, etc.
So, many types of people are trained to perform these disgusting acts in the name of science.
Vivisection is considered quite normal in laboratories.

Now, this is where it links to the alien agenda.

When people started being abducted and experimented on, it was seized upon by a certain group of doctors and biologists as an excuse to abduct animals and humans and blame aliens for the mutilations.

If we may, we will take a page or two to explain this.

There are many branches of science and military who have for a number of years been trying to develop new breeds of humans sometimes called "super soldiers".
However, the term super soldier is misleading.

What misguided scientists, doctors and biologists involved with these practices are attempting to do is a number of things, genetic modification of certain humans for specific tasks.

For instance, the scientific community (this group we are talking about) are aware that, long years ago, a previous race which no longer exists, had mastered the technique of mixing human and animal DNA, not simply to create strange monster entities but to create specific "designer" entities.

Mythological history talks about Sphinx, Minotaur's, Merpeople and on and on.

These are not the random result of mixing horse and human DNA, not the random result of mixing bull, lion and other creatures with human DNA, but the technique had been perfected to create specific creatures according to the design of the geneticists of that time.

The result was creatures that come down to us today in mythology.

Sometimes an entity with a human front end and a horse's rear end - a Centaur - or a man with the head of a bull and so on (a Minotaur).

As you may be aware, genetic experiments on humans, in many countries, is not permitted today, and quite rightly so.

It may have interested the geneticists to tamper with both animal and human genes but the amount of suffering caused to both humans and the animals, the result of these experiments, is beyond calculation.

The strange thing is that the prime directive of medical doctors is not to harm a living creature - the Hippocratic oath, as it is called - but there are secret laboratories all over the world containing medical doctors and skilled biologists that do not think twice before attempting to splice human and animal genes together.

So, let us examine the laboratories that perform these acts and then let us consider why they do this, because you can be sure that there are reasons for these experiments.

Once the genetic code was uncovered (1953), and once contact had been made with evil aliens who offered to share some of their advanced genetic knowledge in exchange for us creating DUMBs and allowing these aliens free access to conduct whatever experiments they wanted to carry out, the door was open, in a sense, to create mixtures of human and animal hybrids.

The medical specialists and the military, in collaboration with some very powerful pharmaceutical companies, realised that the mixing of human and animal DNA was possible because they were fairly sure that it had been done in the past and that certain of these created creatures still survive to this day.

As we mentioned, mixing human and animal genes in a random fashion is hard enough, but to do so with a controlled and repeatable end result, like the previous race of men had achieved, was a different problem altogether.

Thus, in some of these DUMBs and secret areas, experiments were started.
Large numbers of people who would not be missed were and are abducted, physically, and imprisoned in cages in these underground facilities to provide a bank of beings available for experimentation.

Although it is not widely known, humans are not all the same.
The genetic structure alters somewhat depending on the ancestry of the people.

Of the basic races; white, black, yellow, brown skinned, there are slight differences, which needed to be studied and choices made as to which groups would be the most suitable to mix with which animals to create a certain hybrid blend.

Let us now look at the actual mutilation scene.

You must realise that secrecy in these experiments is of the greatest importance, because much of what is being done is strictly illegal and, if discovered and brought to public attention, many heads would roll.
There are secret political groups involved, secret military groups, secret pharmaceutical groups, not to mention what are called three and four letter organisations.

There is great similarity of the level of secrecy of the human/animal hybrid program to the human/alien programme being conducted by evil aliens.

Although the end result is not quite the same, the need for total secrecy is paramount and so humans and aliens work together and share similar bases.

Now, the human geneticists already have a large number of easily physically abducted people of all races stored underground in cages, as we have said, but there was, and is, need to abduct animals to study and experiment on.

It suited both groups, the geneticists and the aliens, to work together to abduct farm animals and, as alien UFOs, in physical form, have the ability to hoist animals into their UFOs, these craft, operated by PLFs, abduct cows, horses, sheep, etc., take them back to the base where experiments are conducted, the necessary DNA and other elements extracted and then the animal is returned to the farm from which it was taken and dropped to the ground by a UFO. Very occasionally helicopters are used for the return journey but helicopters are noisy, slow moving and obviously of Earth origin, so it is preferable to use UFOs, both to take the animals and to return them.

One may ask why the mutilated animals are returned at all?
There are a number of answers to this question.
If an animal just disappeared from a farm, rustlers would be suspected and an expensive investigation conducted.
But, once a three letter agency is aware that a mutilated farm, or even wild, animal is found, they have been warned to hush up the incident and bring any investigation to a halt.

This three letter agency may not be aware of by whom and why these mutilations are being carried out, but they have been made aware that it is top secret and they must get rid of the body and stop any investigation.

So, it is considered that the mutilations are carried out by aliens and, as the alien subject is off topic (not to be mentioned), any investigation immediately stops and so the real perpetrators are safe from disclosure.

So, then the tests on blending human and animal genetics can carry on in secret and no one in the public will be any the wiser.

If you have followed the animal mutilation lectures given by highly respected investigators of the topic, the lectures go round and around showing gory pictures of the mutilated corpses of the animals concerned, then go on to suggest alien interference as the source and then the lecture stops.
In other words, the lectures are always just a repeat of what is known; mutilated corpses and tales of farmers seeing UFOs and that is all.
There is never any talk of what the real cause is because, either the lecturer is ignorant of the reason why they take place, or they are frightened of being assassinated for revealing any truth on the subject.

We feel that the public has the right to know what is going on but we also protect the people who work with us in revealing these horrors.

So, let us progress as far as we can.

We mentioned that the concept behind animal abductions is to create hybrid monsters, a blend of human and animal.
We mentioned that large numbers of people are abducted and kept in cages in DUMBs, so that a range of all different DNA types of people are available for experimentation.
Plus, of course, many different animal body parts are stored in these DUMBs and, in very secret areas of the DUMBs, scientists are performing experiments, sometimes on their own and sometimes being helped by aliens.

The results of these experiments, if alive, are stored in areas deep underground.
You may have heard people talk of Nightmare Hall in one of these DUMBs.
People talk of seeing humans horribly disfigured with part human, part animal aspects to them.
These are the results of the experiments that take place in attempts to create human/animal hybrids.
The people who have seen Nightmare Hall, and talk about it, mention PLFs there also, caring for the needs of these experiments: food, drink, cleaning the cages and administering any drugs needed either to keep these poor creatures alive or to keep them sedated.
So, they put two and two together and come to the wrong conclusion that all this is being done by aliens as part of their agenda - whatever that might be.

Of course, they have no idea of the truth that these foul experiments are actually part of a human agenda to create animal/human hybrids.

The question one must eventually address is, 'What exactly are they trying to create?' After all humans are clever people, where as animals are considered dumb beasts, so what could possibly be the advantage of blending a human with an animal?

Actually, there are a number of reasons, most of them with military connections - on the face of it at least - which enables the organisations promoting all this to get funding from the taxpayer via what are known as "black budget" methods of concealing where money is going and what it is used for.

You must be aware that to set up such a vast organisation creating human/animal hybrids in total secrecy for such a long period of time and, at the same time, hide the alien agenda, is a vast and complex security problem. A problem which is only resolved by pouring massive amounts of money and resources into keeping every aspect totally compartmentalised so that only a few evil, but trusted, individuals are aware of the truth.

Should the truth of the reality of the scale of these operations ever be revealed to the public, the majority of humanity would deny that it was, and is, possible.

Of course, the fact that most decent people naturally do not want to believe that such things are possible, aids enormously the people concerned with security to maintain secrecy.

Most people are aware of the myths of the various creatures that come down to us from the past and are used in a number of books and films to entertain the public, but few, indeed, would be prepared to accept that the same, or similar, creatures are being created just under their feet in these secret hideaways.

So high is the level of secrecy that many, indeed most, of the people employed in the genetic manipulation scenario are unaware of what is going on.
The trick with all this is because of the very clever ruse called compartmentalization.

Can you imagine, for a moment, the vast number of people involved in just creating a DUMB?
Obviously, people are employed to design a DUMB.
Then contractors are brought in to dig the site.
Then a vast number of outside contractors are employed to create all that is necessary to furnish the DUMB with huge amounts of highly specialised and specially developed materials such as elevators (lifts), alarm systems, cages of all sorts, storage areas, laboratories of incredibly advanced types, food storage, restaurants, bedrooms … the list goes on and on.
And all this manufactured, transported to the site and installed, without anyone working on the project having the faintest idea of what is going on, what they are manufacturing and installing and why they are doing it.

Then, scientists of many types are employed to carry out the DNA experiments.

We must consider the enormous infrastructure needed to keep a DUMB operating. Electricity, gas, water and many other elements gathered from all over the world and taken to the DUMB when required.

Also, transport of personnel and materials, a host of security guards, a host of caterers and so on.

A DUMB is a veritable underground city with, eventually, thousands of people involved in one way or another and financed, secretly, by funds syphoned from the tax system.

Thanks to this compartmentalization, the secret is maintained.
The system is simple and works like this.

Above a DUMB is usually created a small series of buildings holding security personnel and a few military and Air Force people to give the semblance of a military base of some sort.
Let us take a small, almost laughable, example.
Bread.

An order goes to one or, usually, more than one bakery firm to provide a certain number of loaves of bread each day.
Often, the order is split and goes to a number of bakery factories somewhat remote from the base.

Now, on their own, the orders are for relatively small numbers of loaves, so as not to raise suspicion but, collectively, the amount of bread ordered each day would be enormous.

The orders come from the military and the baker is instructed to bake X amount of loaves each day.
Then, quite often, a truck will arrive at the factory, loads up and drives to a depot.
So that is all the baker is aware of.

The transport company just knows that, each day, they must collect X loaves and deliver them to a site, where they are unloaded.
That is as far as the transport company is concerned.

But the same thing is going on from a number of bakers spread around America, or the country concerned.
Then the loaves are transported to a larger site and loaded onto a plane and flown to a landing strip close to the DUMB - of which there is no evidence over ground except the few buildings that were mentioned earlier. Once again, the crew of the plane may not be

aware of what they are carrying as the loaves would be wrapped and placed on pallets to hide what they are.

From the landing strip, these anonymous creates or packages would be stored and other people would arrive to take them to a huge elevator, or lift.

Others who would lower them down the elevator and yet others, underground, would transport them on and on until, finally, they end up in a number of restaurants underground where people eat - but each group separately.

The security guards do not eat with the scientists. Even the top scientists seldom mix with those lower down the genetic program.

Thus, we hope you can see that even for a simple loaf of bread a vast amount of precaution is taken to ensure secrecy.

It is referred to as compartmentalization. This rather uncouth word is at the heart of the security program for both the human and alien agenda.

As a safeguard, should anything be revealed, blame is put upon the aliens working in these DUMBs and who have far above top secret level of protection from investigation.

So, let us now consider some of the motives for creating human/animal hybrids.

First, we should repeat what we have already mentioned and it is this.

The geneticists at the top of the program know that strange beings were created a long time ago by an advanced race who no longer exist.

But the geneticists who met and discussed this event with certain military today, realised that if such creatures existed and were created long ago, the scientists of that time must have had good reason.

Further, the alien hybrid agenda was known about and it was hoped that the modern-day geneticists could ask the Greys to assist in the development of human/animal creations because the military were helping the Greys with their program of creating human/alien hybrids.

The Greys agreed to this and so the program was organised without any clear objective of where it might take them.

Of course, the background thought was always military advantage.

It was thought that if it were possible, for example, to create a creature with the strength of a bull but the brains of a human, that would definitely be a formidable weapon on the battlefield.

Of course, the animal would need to be changed quite a lot.

A bull might have formidable strength but if it did not have human type arms, it could not hold a weapon.

Also, the brain of the human would have to be altered just to obey orders but have no concept of disobeying any orders.

So much cogitation went on as to how to proceed.

Would it be possible to grow a bull with a human head?

Would it be possible to grow a bull with an extra pair of arms like a Centaur?

What level of intelligence would it need?

How could its natural instincts be suppressed? For instance, should these bull/human hybrids be lined up on the battlefield and the enemy passed a drone and sprayed "cow in heat" hormones into a distant pasture, a normal bull would lose all interest in what it was doing, charge after the hormone smell and start to battle with the other bulls present for the right to mate with the supposed female.

These sorts of instincts obviously needed to be suppressed.

Exactly what type of hybrid the scientists hope for is not really the subject of this discussion.

It is the fact that humans and animals were and are being abducted, experimented on (vivisection) in the vain hopes of constructing the correct genetic code to create such a beast, is what really interests us.

It is the degree of human and animal suffering that concerns us.

We are also concerned at the level of deceit being used and the vast financial and other resources being siphoned off. Resources that could and should be used to better people's lives: care for the sick, care for the homeless, food for all, etc.

Let us go on to say that the Archangels, directed by God to put the logos of life into anything (or not), reluctantly put a soul with these creatures as they are both - human and animal - creatures from Earth initially, created by God and do not contain any alien parts.

So, the poor wretched creatures created in laboratories and stored in cages deep underground are truly alive, just as we (you and I) are.

In our eyes, it is an abomination against God to create such creatures.

If the Directors of Life had decided that they were necessary, they would have made them long ago.

Further, one could question if such creatures would really be necessary in a peaceful civilisation, which is the direction in which we are heading?

As these creatures are truly alive, it might be possible that they could breed between themselves. If this were to be the case, what do we do with the offspring?

So, we can only wait and see what these modern scientists come up with.

One can be sure that every type of creature that myths are made of from long ago will be envisaged: Merpeople, Centaurs, Minotaur's and everything that is shown in fantasy films today.

Indeed, when one sees the types of monsters shown in some films, one wonders if knowledge of these experiments is not being leaked to certain filmmakers to help prepare us for the day these creatures are shown publicly.

After all, it was done with the UFO phenomenon and people accept that there are UFOs and PLFs now with little surprise.

Like with all these chapters, we could go on and fill pages with what we are aware of concerning this program, which is still in its infancy.
But, the question concerning animal mutilations, we have answered and clearly explained that, although there is alien help given, the program that results in these mutilations has been addressed. It is of human origin.

It is up to you now to consider what we have said and either believe what we have told you or go on thinking that it is just Grey aliens who are behind these events.

CHAPTER 15

TIME TRAVEL

This next chapter will examine another aspect considered part of the alien agenda which is time travel.

This subject has never been understood, like so much of what is called wisdom or collective consciousness concerning this strange subject - alien life.
We have had to explain to you that the vast majority of so-called knowledge concerning aliens has been misunderstood and that, in fact, most of the events attributed to aliens are actually coming from aspects of humans in one way or another either connected to humans incarnate or discarnate.

We have no doubt that many of you will be struggling to comprehend what we have so far said, as it flies in the face of anything you may have previously heard or learned concerning aliens and/or animal mutilations.

But this chapter will take us onto a version of life that is known about but not understood.

Many of you will be aware of so-called aliens pretending to have come from some aspect of the future - often in Grey form - asking permission to abduct humans today to cure some genetic defect that occurred at some time in their future that is causing humanity in the future to die out.
Of course, a moment's thought would indicate that this is probably a cock and bull story, if you will forgive the expression, and that Grey aliens wish for permission to abduct humans for a completely different reason connected to creating alien/human hybrids. Thus, these aliens would be coming from our time and not the future at all.

Then, of course, there are stories of ordinary humans that claim to be time travellers and spend their time travelling around the world moving from time period to time period. Once again, these stories are difficult to believe as the information they give does not seem to throw much light on any advanced technology that might exist in the future and that they could explain to us.

We have one or two cases of people having been in contact either with aliens or spacecraft from the future and the person contacted received a mass of binary code of one form or another indicating that the UFO in question came from the future.

We could go on giving examples from popular culture concerning time travel or time travelers.

Then, of course, we have the opposite camp who claim that time travel is not possible and will cover blackboards with masses of mathematics to demonstrate that time travel is impossible.

One classic example given is that if time travel was possible and someone came back from the future, it would mean that the future has already happened.

If we may explain this from another aspect, imagine that we were able to travel from today back in time either a short while or a vast length of time.
Now, we can imagine travelling back in time because the past has already happened and is set in stone so to speak.
But, if we regard today from the point of view of sometime in the past, it presents a problem in that from today, if we had the ability, we could, in theory, trace each day and note events, in note books, back and back, day by day, second by second, if we had the ability to note that much, back to some point in the past.

Once we arrived at our destination time in the past, we would have a pile of notebooks and could demonstrate to a person in the past exactly what was going to happen, day by day, or second by second as we moved forward from the past back to today (now).

If it was possible to do this, it would demonstrate that, from the point of view of the past, the future has (had) already happened and we would have a pile of notebooks to prove it.

But then, if we scratch our heads we find a flaw in the logic.
If someone had the ability to note in a notebook the main events occurring around the world, not only today but at this precise moment you are reading these words, but went back to yesterday, he should have no record of today - from yesterday's point of view - as today has not happened from the point of view of yesterday so nothing would have been noted in the notebook.

Can you see the conundrum? We can trace, from today, events that occurred in the past but, unless the future has already happened, from the past we cannot trace any future event.

It gives the impression that time only travels in one direction, from the past to the future. Or rather from now to the future.

If that were so, no one could come from the future because from the point of view of the past, the future does not exist and so, if someone travelled to the past he would cease to exist because he comes from sometime in the future that has not yet happened so he is not yet born so could not go back to the past. He can only go on from now.

This seems to be a circular argument and, if we just accept that as true - that time only moves from this moment on into the future, second by second - there is no point in going on and so we could end this chapter here and just say that time travel is not possible.
And there are people who think that, but for others they have a deep feeling that there is more to time than that and it should be possible to move back and forth in time.
So how do we investigate this, intelligently, to find the answer?

Let us start by repeating that which we have already explained.

We have said that time is made of billions of still frames of time each second, each one connected to a past or future frame, rather like looking at a cine film.

Logically, the past frames have been exposed and contain images but the future frames would be unexposed and contain no images, as the future has not happened.

We know that this is a difficult concept if you have not heard of it before but we ask you to accept it if you can for the sake of argument.

We also said that each frame is stored in the living library that we call the Akashic Record.

So, if we examine the Akashic Records we can see recordings of all people, all events occurring anywhere in the multiverse and going back from now, endlessly into the past.

We have also said that each frame is protected with a code that prevents anyone from altering the past and have said that if someone watches events that have happened in the past, he will be watching a copy of the events and not the original.

The copy can be altered but that would not affect the actual recording, which will remain unalterable for all time.

But we have also mentioned the Mandela effect, where certain events today seem not to be as we remember from the past.

If you read our essay on the Mandela effect, we mentioned that this happens because all is illusion and only seems real by popular belief - acceptance that something is real.

But, we also said that if popular belief (universal consciousness) alters, events in the past can alter.

So, the story gets more and more complicated.

However, logically there should be an answer to the question, 'Does time travel exist?'

If we analyse correctly all the known wisdom on the subject it should lead us to an answer, either:

1. Yes, time travel exists, or
2. No, it does not exist.

The secret with all true investigation, is to keep an open mind, have no preconceived notion of which outcome we expect, investigate and see where the evidence leads us.

All too often, people start any and all questions, whatever the subject, with a notion of which answer they want or expect and, lo and behold, their investigations prove them correct.

It is obvious that, by the Law of Mutual Attraction, if we have already made up our minds concerning a subject, then we will draw towards us information that reinforces the original concept.

Scientific truth has gone out of the window.

The problem has always been this.
Science is based on past teachings but past teachings may or may not be correct.

Many people have great respect for the many professors who have received Nobel prizes for some original thought that has been presented to an amazed public and certainly we would not diminish the achievements of these people but, if one looks back over the person's past education career, with very few exceptions, one can trace an educational path where the professor's brain, when young, had been stuffed with conventional scientific or philosophical knowledge dating back, in certain cases, hundreds, if not thousands of years.

Thus, from that springboard, the professor launches himself into what he hopes are new discoveries.

The problem is that we end up today with the written teachings of these old masters, whatever their field, but we cannot know the context in which they lived and worked which, inevitably, must have colored their thoughts at that time, just as our society colors the thinking of today's geniuses.

Thus, it is we have, today, many highly qualified, highly respected scientists, mathematicians and physicists, that state categorically that aliens do not exist, for example, despite the fact that UFOs are seen in the skies daily and a large number of people are working in various places with aliens - or their robots - daily.

Once again, our old friend the Law of Mutual Attraction is at work, bringing truth to those who seek truth and illusion to those who seek illusion.

The point we are making is that, to find any truth, all we can do is to study the evidence with an open mind and see where it takes us.

In the case of time travel, the problem is further complicated by a number of factors.

The only way to prove that time travel is possible, is to do it.
But, would you be prepared to launch yourself, blindly, into the past or the future with no safety net, no guarantee of being able to come back to "now"?

And even if you were brave enough to take the plunge, how would you prove to the world that you really went somewhere?
Even if you brought back some artefact with you, you would be accused of fraud.

Don't forget, if people are convinced that time travel is not possible, nothing that you could do or show them would convince them otherwise.

Then, for those who know that we are not just physical beings but have a large, non-physical aspect to us, which part of that duplex do we use; just the physical part, just the non-physical part or all of it - body and soul - so to speak?

We could go on but we hope you can see that time travel, unless and until it is fully and safely mastered, is a tricky concept.

It rather reminds us, in a totally unrelated way, to the somewhat amusing argument about how did an eye develop.

We all, or most of us, have eyes.
But how did they develop?
You can't have a bit of an eye. You can't have half an eye. You need to have, from the beginning, a fully working eye, complete with all its neural connections to the brain or it would not make sense.

Certainly, we can examine birds, fish and other aquatic mammals and see the remnants of arms and legs, hands and feet but, as far as we are concerned, no prehistoric creature has ever been discovered with an early form of an eye.
Creatures seemed either to have eyes or they did not.
They may not have looked exactly like our eyes but they are, or were, fully functioning eyes nevertheless.

Time machines must surely be the same. Either a machine will take one back and forth in time or it won't.

We have spent several pages examining the pros and cons of time travel and have exposed to you some of the problems concerning time travel but have not yet addressed the subject matter of this chapter, which is time travel.

We felt that it would be beneficial to discuss what the various arguments are concerning the two questions we asked (is time travel possible or not), so as to expose to you that it is very much a fraught question, which is to say a question not easy to answer, unless one experiences it oneself.

We have examined the facts demonstrating that time travel is impossible, which was not hard to do because, on the face of it, time travel would present so many difficulties that it is easier to dismiss the whole affair as lunacy and stop at that.

But, just as we hope that we have been able to demonstrate that aliens and UFOs are real by being able to step outside of conventional physics and collective wisdom and, looking at the question from a different point of view - which happens to be the correct answer to the alien question - so, perhaps, if we look at time travel from a different angle, it might shed some light on the subject.
But, please remember that we are not seeking to prove that time travel is possible, we are just examining possibilities.

So, we know that to seek answers from a physical standpoint will get us nowhere, so we have no alternative but to seek within the non-physical.

If you have followed our various talks and read the literature we have put at your disposal, you will know that the non-physical is a veritable Pandora's box of possibilities. But we must open that box and see what flies out. Who knows, we might find a clue!

Our knowledge of esoteric matters suggests to us that it would be reasonable to seek within dimensions and/or alternative realities.

We have a fairly comprehensive knowledge concerning both these aspects of life and so we should be able to sift through them fairly rapidly and hone in on any likely avenues for exploration.

We are going to apologise to you at this point because we are sure that many of you have already guessed that time travel is possible and that we know how it works and yet we have spent quite a lot of time gently approaching the moment when we can tell you how it works but our teaching wisdom, amassed over long years, tells us that it is better to approach an unusual and perhaps revolutionary subject slowly to allow all, from the brightest student to the slowest, to be able to understand. All have the right to know. Not just the brightest.

We have decided between us (our group of the Great White Brotherhood), whether we should go on explaining or whether we should jump to the bare facts of the matter, at the risk of losing some of you.
We have decided to take the plunge, explain how time travel works and rely on anyone lost to do their homework with our other publications to fill in the gaps.

So, we wish to say that time travel is possible because all is one.
There are not huge numbers of people spread over vast eons of time.
There is one consciousness and one moment in time (now).
All else is illusion.

We hope that for those who know what we are talking about, this will make sense and start to make you realise how this affects time travel.

For those of you who have no idea what we are talking about, we suggest that you stop here and go to the material we have already given you and sift through it until you do understand.
We did not want to insult anyone by spending a lot of time and effort explaining again what we have already explained.

But, we will expand on the concept as far as consideration that there is only one consciousness and only one moment of time.

Let us examine the reality behind the illusion, that there are countless people spread over eons of time is concerned.

Although we have said that we are all given personal aspects that make us feel individual, we have also said behind this is the concept that we are all just one aspect of consciousness.

If this is true it implies that you, Julius Caesar, Moses and all the other people from the past, present and future, are just one single consciousness.
We can't even really call that consciousness a person.

Let us give a simple example. Imagine that we take a single drop of water and place it on a saucer or something. Then we take another drop of water and place it on another saucer and so on.
But then, if we combined them together in one saucer, the drops lose their individuality and become combined.
Then, if we take this now larger drop of water and place it in a huge lake or a sea, the individual drops lose all their individual identities and become one huge "drop", if we can call a sea a drop of water.

The point we are making is that a sea consists of countless drops of water that have combined to make a collective whole, which is what is called a sea.

It is the same with consciousness. Individually, we have the impression that there are countless people (consciousnesses) but, collectively there is only one.

Now, let us consider time.
Once again, on a physical level, all is illusion.
We imagine that time comes from the past, passes by a fleeting "now" moment and … in a way stops there waiting for the next moment to arrive.

But the reality is that time is made of countless "now" moments.

Consider a cine film. A projector is loaded with a huge roll of undeveloped film.

Then, as a scene is acted and the camera turns, one frame comes into view of the lens and a snapshot is taken, then the mechanism turns and the second frame of film lines up with the lens and a second snapshot is taken.
Thus, it progresses on and on.
If we view the film, once it is developed, we see that what appears on the silver screen as a moving picture is, in fact, a number of "now" moments - snapshots - joined together and made to pass through a projector at a certain number of frames, 12, 24, 48 frames/ second or whatever.

Life is rather like that but on a cosmos scale.
Just a series of now moments, that we view as time.

But, time is very difficult to describe in simple terms because people do not, generally, understand time.

If time is just "now", how can time exist?
Why are we not stuck in a never ending repeat of "now", just repeating over and over again?

Well, in a way we are but consciousness never stands still and so, despite the fact that time is just now, the wheel of consciousness can propel us forward or backwards as a consciousness decides to look at a moment of so-called time.
We have said that time does not really exist but sequence of events does.

You can probably remember what you were doing five minutes ago or an hour ago or a week ago or back to your early childhood.

You may not remember all the events, second by second, but you can remember events that stick out in the recent or distant past.

But, if we go back to our example of the drop of water in a sea, some might be far out to sea, deep in the water, some might be on the surface, rising and falling as waves.
Some of them might be crashing onto a shore somewhere.
Others might be ingested by the gills of a fish.

All have individual experiences but, together constitute an ocean.

Therefore, we hope that you can see that each drop of water is having individual experiences but, together, all the drops of water constitute what we call a sea or an ocean.

We hope that you can see that your individual consciousness is really connected to all consciousnesses, past, present and future and becomes one.

The difference is that whereas a drop of water does not have the ability to choose in which part of the ocean to be, as it is at the mercy of wind and tide, you do.

You can decide to move back and forth, not exactly in time but in experience.

You can move your "now" moment.
Either you may remain in the "now" moment, as most people do, and let fate, your life plan, unfold as it will or you can move to another "now" moment that we call the past or the future.

But you cannot do this in 3D physicality. You can do it using your non-physical aspect that we call consciousness.

Actually, as we have already explained at great length, your physical experience is just an illusion and you are just a point of consciousness pretending to have a physical experience. So, if you move to another point in time, you will experience it as real. You will see that you have a body, even though your 3D body will be sitting on a chair here on Earth.

So, in effect, you will have created a second body.

The first one, that you consider to be the real you, will still be on Earth and be subject to all the reality of the Earth experience; heat, cold, hunger, thirst and so on, while another aspect of your consciousness will be away somewhere exploring the past or the future. But, this second body will seem just as real as your first, except that you will not be subject to hot and cold, etc.

You will be in astral form (which is the real you anyway).

Once you have finished exploring the past or the future, you will immediately return to your physical body.

This is of course, what happens when people do Astral Projection, or what people who meditate correctly and are taken to trips to heaven do.

The physical body remains on Earth and another aspect of consciousness wanders off to the past or the future.

Actually, if one develops this faculty of directing another aspect of consciousness to another part of the astral realms, there is virtually no limit to what one can do, where one can go and what one can experience.

All this is possible because all the events over all of time and in all dimensions are created as one point, but it is a point that one can open, using one's sense of individuality, allowing the person to explore anywhere.

Imagine, for example, a huge castle and you have permission to explore all of it.

You may wander about going from room to room and watching the activities going on in each room, from the kitchens to the living rooms and so on.

Now, once we really master the secret (it is not really a secret) of how to project an aspect of consciousness into the astral realms, there is no limit.

You may remember Jesus said, 'my father's house has many mansions.' This is what he was referring to.

Now, if we may go on, you can probably see that the past would be fairly easy to explore, as would aspects of the present.
But what about the future?

In theory, the future does not exist and in physicality that is true.
But, as all is one, logically, on another level, the future must exist.

And so, it does, but not exactly as one timeline.

If we examine the past, we should also realise that there was no "one" experience.
Each and every person that ever lived had an individual experience.
History books portray a series of events as if all life was just one thing.

We learn about the Romans, early man in many countries, the capture of America by the Spanish, slavery, abolition of slavery and so on, as if it was all just a series of events, just following one after another but, in reality, history contains the personal experiences of all people over time.

In order to really recount history correctly, the writers of history books would have to recount the personal story of each and every person at a particular time and explain how those personal events molded the next level of events as life unfolded.
Countless numbers of people, together, create what, in history books is explained in a few pages: the Roman occupation of countries, the Spanish occupation of America and so on. The books totally ignore the day by day, minute by minute experiences that each and every person went through to create what is described in history books.

This is perfectly understandable, of course, because (a) the historians have no ability to contact the life experiences of all the individuals concerned and (b) any such book would be impossibly large.

So, historians just garner together what evidence they can and present an overall picture of an event.
But, in reality, each and every moment of time constitutes the experiences of all the people alive at that moment.

So, if we try to go into the future, there is no such thing as "the future" as such.
It will always be the collective experience of all the people alive all over the world at any particular moment.

So, it is possible to go a little way into the future but as people react to events, the timeline alters rather like driving down a road.

Imagine that you drive down the road not knowing where you are going.
Eventually you will come to a fork in the road. Do you turn left, right or go straight on? Whatever decision you decide to make, you will eventually come to another fork and then another.
Can you see that from the place you start out, you could end up anywhere?

Exploring the future is very much like that. There is not just one future. There are countless futures and, as one advances, the future becomes more and more hazy and uncertain, until it is impossible to continue, impossible to make any sense of it as there will be an incredible number of possibilities, depending on the life experiences of all future people.

We wish to emphasize that if you time travel, it would be your consciousness that will be travelling but, as life only exists because of the personal consciousness of countless individuals, if they were not there, the past or the future would not exist.
It is all these consciousnesses that create events.

Imagine a beehive. It works and honey is produced because the bees - the living creatures - create the hive. Without the bees, the hive would have no meaning.

It is the same with the past, present or future.
They exist as concepts but it is all the people, animals, plants and minerals that actually create events.

Without people to experience it, the past, present or future would be meaningless, sterile blocks of nothingness.
It is people that bring the past, present and future to life.

So, although we might visit one of these times, it is the fact that there are people there that give it credibility and we would link with someone and see the past or the future through their eyes, so to speak.

It is not exactly like that but, as we are all one, we can link with someone of that time, past or future, and experience what he experiences.

We can, if we know how, change from one person to another and experience what more than one person sees.

Therefore, time travel is possible but, unless you have a firm idea of who and what you want to see at some precise moment in the future and have developed the competence to get to that exact spot, at that moment in time and linked with that person, you will finish up in a haze of possibilities rather like a drop of water in an ocean that is just washing about as the life of the ocean unfolds.

So, we suggest that you be careful with time travel and with people who report coming from the past or future in physical form.
They may not be telling the truth.

Now, the actual technique for learning to do time travel is easy.
It is just meditation.

If you meditate correctly for a few minutes each day, you will fill your auras with spiritual power, that will enable you to do a number of things, among them being able to move into the past or future.

Making sense of what you see there is another matter.

What you will find out if you explore the past, is that much of what is written in history books is not exactly correct, at best, and downright fabrication at worst.

It has been said that history is written by the vainqueurs and this is largely true.

So, if you take the time and effort to learn time travel, do not expect to come back with any startling revelations. Certainly, future people will have different technologies and certainly life will be better in the future than it is today but, for most people, life just goes on and people live it much as they do today.

People are people and accept life as they find it to be, so there are new and better things in the future but what you experience will depend on who you link with. It might be someone in a city or it might be some native living in a jungle.

There maybe anti-gravity vehicles on so on but, as you will be linking with the consciousness of the people of whatever time you arrive at, it will seem as normal as seeing a car is to most people today.

So, we have explained that time travel in astral form is possible - but not physical - so although anyone can learn to do it, it is, in our opinion, largely a waste of time and it would be better to concentrate one's efforts in improving life now… today!

CHAPTER 16

SPACE TRAVEL

This chapter will discuss the pros and cons of space travel.

We must remember that we have two sorts of aliens and thus two sorts of spacecraft. You will remember that we said that the first group, that we termed the true aliens and are actually aspects of us that we gave the rather unwieldy term "personality bundles" to and the second sort are created under the auspices of demonic forces from the lower fourth dimension that we termed the Greys.

Now, we also said that the craft grown in astral form by the true aliens are grown, rather like a foetus is grown in the womb of a female, and is largely human in concept and that is living and has a soul just as you do, plus all the attributes that a living creature has, except that it is not designed to have a physical incarnation.
We will expand on this as we proceed.

The second group of UFOs are physically created here on Earth and we will expand on that also.

So, this chapter will be in two parts.

If we may, we will begin by examining the craft that come from the true aliens first.

You may remember us telling you that this group are actually unused "personality bundles", one of eight personality aspects that we all have and are unused, as our main focus is on one aspect of reality, whether we are incarnate or discarnate, leaving the other seven aspects of personality to their own devices.

Now, although we did our best to explain to you what personality bundles are, we do appreciate that it is a difficult concept to appreciate and we don't expect all people to accept blindly what we have said.

However, it happens to be the truth and so we can only report the truth to you and let you accept or reject this strange concept.

Also, hard to accept is that these personality bundles can either choose to follow you around, although you are only making use of one of them, so they would just follow you around pointlessly or they can decide to do something or become something, until you decide to switch from one bundle to another, in which case one of them would drop what he/she is doing and be at your service.
Of course, that would leave the first bundle free to do something to pass the time!

We also said that, to a certain extent, it depends on the level of intelligence of the person and his personality as to whether the personality bundles feel like acting on their own or not.

We will expand on this as it has a bearing on spaceships.

As you will know, there are many types of people, some very intelligent, some not very intelligent, some very kind and some quite evil.
By the Law of Mutual Attraction, an intelligent person with great curiosity would create personality bundles intelligent and with curiosity.

Then, there are those at the opposite end of the scale who are not at all intelligent and do not, generally, have much curiosity, just doing what they do, draw their pay at the end of the week and watch TV when not at work.
Obviously, these people's personality bundles reflect that sort of person.

Now, please do not think that we are criticizing such people, because we are not.
People without much intelligence are very valuable to society.

We need people to clean the streets, empty the trash cans and do the 101 menial tasks that civilisation needs to be done.

If an intelligent person was tasked with cleaning out blocked drains all day, he would soon revolt and would do the job badly, but if a non-intelligent person is asked to do the same job, he would do it with pride and do it well.
So, we very much need non-intelligent people and they are usually well received when their lifespan finishes and they return home to heaven.
They are usually gentle, kind and considerate people - attributes very much sought after in heaven - and they are nurtured and cared for in heaven, because they are often a lot more spiritual than highly intelligent people who can suffer from inflated egos - attributes frowned upon in heaven.
Humility and willingness to serve are what heaven looks for. Not inflated egos.

We would like to repeat something concerning people at opposite ends of the social scale that we have mentioned before but is worth repeating.

It is considered that a king, queen, prince, president or whomever is more important than someone who empties people's trash cans (dustbins) and cleans the roads.
They are paid enormous sums of money, live in magnificent palaces and are generally cared for at the highest level.
Meanwhile the trash people just go about their business in all weathers, disposing of garbage.

Please consider this. If a king went on strike, what would be the effect on the general population? None we would suggest.
However, if trash people went on strike, the effect is immediate.

Mountains of stinking garbage piling up in the streets causing, in hot weather, health problems.

Thus, for the population that the king purports to serve or a trashman who serves the community, who is the most important?

We suggest that a trashman is the most important and, when his incarnation is finished and he goes to the heavenly realms, he is heartily applauded by the angelic spirits who followed his incarnation.

On the other hand, many a king, queen, prince, or president arriving in heaven and expecting to be treated with the same deference that they had on Earth, have been shocked to have their many faults revealed to them and even more shocked to find that they have to spend time in the dismal realms, purging themselves of their many ego driven faults.

In the meantime, the trashman is basking in the beauty of heaven, having a just reward for all the long years of service he gave to his community.

There is a lesson there that many could retain.

So, never look down at those who do menial jobs.
This service is vital for a community.

But let us go back to the personality bundles that we all have.

A person who has little intelligence may not have much curiosity either.
His various personality bundles would, in all probability, not have much curiosity also.
They tend to content themselves just with following the person around.
This is fine.
There is nothing wrong with this but, we suggest that they would not be the sorts of personalities that would wish to become aliens and explore planet Earth.

So, in all probability, it is the personalities of more intelligent, curious people that would seek experience apart from the person incarnate or discarnate.

This is actually a good thing, as curiosity - like necessity when incarnate - is the mother of invention in the astral realms.
In non-physicality we want for nothing, but if we don't have curiosity it is impossible to advance any project.

Everything in non-physicality is produced by thought and curiosity provokes thought on a project.

So, those personality bundles that wanted to explore Earth, quickly realised that they would need a craft of some sort in order to appear in 3D Earth skies.

However, the problem is that in non-physicality, metals, plastics and all the things that would be necessary to create a 3D spacecraft do not exist.

Everything is astral, which is to say that it is an aspect of consciousness.
Consciousness is also vibration which is a subset of light - the starlight of God.

But, it was also realised that if a craft could be made, it would also be made of vibration - the same frequency as the dimension in which it would be conceived.
It was also realised that vibration can be manipulated and if it were possible to create a spacecraft, as it vibrates, it would be a fairly simple process of altering the frequency to the frequency of the 6th dimension, which is where you live, and thus it would appear in the 6th dimension.
As the ship would then be vibrating to the frequency of the 6th dimension, which seems solid to you, the ship would appear solid.

Now, as we have already explained earlier, when altering frequency, it is not the original object that changes frequency, a copy is created identical to the original.

So, if this were to be done, we would, in fact, have two spaceships.
The first one would remain in the original dimension and the second one would be a carbon copy of the original but of a different frequency (that of the 6th dimension).

We have said that when someone on Earth decides to go to a different dimension, his physical body remains on Earth, while his consciousness creates a copy corresponding to the frequency of the dimension he wishes to visit.

A spacecraft would be much the same.
However, the operative word is consciousness.
If something or someone does not have consciousness - which is actually another word for life - it cannot do this trick of creating of copy of itself to explore another dimension.

So, a spaceship must be alive at this level.
Grey ships are different, as we will explain.

So, the task was how to create a spaceship that is alive.

We break off here just to say that we have abandoned the term "unidentified flying object", UFO, because what we are talking about here is something that has been identified and is not an object, it is a living, thinking being.

So, although we entitled this chapter "Space Travel", it is important to understand what a spaceship is at this level or you would not understand what we are talking about when we get around to describing space travel.

Thus, it was deemed necessary to create a vehicle that was alive and get the seal of approval from the Archangels to get a life Logos put with it.

We would like to say that no computer, no Artificial Intelligence machine will ever be alive, as it will never be given the seal of approval by the Archangels who work for God and have the authority to put a life Logos with anything.
If it does not have certain attributes, it will not pass the test and so will not be given a Logos by the Archangels.

So, it was deemed necessary to create a living space ship from… nothing but thought!

Can you imagine how difficult this must have been?
We should also say that a number of personality bundles got together to work on this project.

We have also stated in other publications that it is not in the purview of man to create life.
It comes from God and is given to a person, animal or whatever by the Archangels and is called the Logos of God (the seal of authority to be alive).

So, these personality bundles looked about and they noticed that there were countless atoms floating about in astral form and wondered if it were possible to persuade some of these atoms to form a spaceship in the astral worlds.

As you know, each and every atom is not just randomly floating about.
Each atom was created to be part of something, whether that something was human, animal, mineral or space and in all dimensions.

So, as the astral personality bundles would obviously need high intellect and also the atoms required to make an advanced spaceship to be intelligent, a call went out to see if some personality bundles - not being used by people - would care to become spaceships for a while.

Now, we realise that this reads like a fairy-tale, but bare with us and see if it makes sense at the end.
You can always reject all this if you want but please follow the explanation to the end and see how you feel then.

As you will also know, in the astral realms, everything is immortal and everything has free will.
So, if a personality bundle let himself be transformed into a spaceship, it was not that dramatic as it sounds because, in the astral realms, everything is basically light - vibration - and so if a ball of astral light is transformed into something, it still remains the consciousness that it was before.

We don't know if you can follow this because we don't have the equivalent in physicality, so we cannot give an appropriate example.

We could just use, for example, a ball of clay.
If we take a ball of clay and create an object from it, it still remains the same ball of clay but transformed.
If, eventually, you did not want what you had created, you could always take the clay and reform it into a ball again.

Perhaps we could use another example; Origami.
One takes a sheet of paper, folds it and if you have the skill, you can make the paper look like a "something", a bird, a plane or whatever.
But is still remains a sheet of paper.

But, what we are trying to express is that the personality bundle that volunteered to be molded into an astral spaceship, would not in any way lose his original concept. He would just take a different shape for a while.
He could always return to his original form at any time if he wished.
Now you either accept this explanation or reject it but that is basically what an astral spaceship is.

It is a personality bundle not being used by someone, that has volunteered to become an astral spaceship.

It is a sobering thought that, perhaps, one of your unused personality aspects is playing at being a spaceship!
The same would apply to anyone of us, of course.

Now, the question is how were these spaceships manufactured in the astral realms?
The answer comes from the Akashic Record.

There were, at one time or another, very advanced races on Earth that had developed space travel.
These races had been systemically wiped out, usually by "elimination level events" (ELE) - asteroids smashing into Earth - but we must also say that there is evidence that, long ago, there was a form of nuclear war that destroyed most of life.
Life on Earth gradually builds up again with the help of the Directors of Life and starts again.

So, as the Akashic Record is not affected by any ELE event, just recording it, it was possible for the personality bundles to travel back through the record until they came across a race that had developed space travel on Earth and copy the plans.

We insist on reminding you once again that a personality bundle is exactly as alive as you are and has access to all the elements that you have: Higher Self, Imagination, etc.

The only difference is, that you who are reading this book, have been programmed to think that you are in physicality, while your personality bundle remains in astral form.

So, it was not too difficult to create an astral version of an advanced spaceship that had been created by an advanced race on Earth long ago.

The actual plans may not have been drawn in the Akashic Record but the thoughts of the inventors were, so it was fairly easy to piece it all together.

As a personality bundle has, in association with it, all the atoms, in astral form, that anyone in physicality has and, as a personality bundle had volunteered to take part in this project, the astral forms of all, or many, of the atoms in association, were gathered together and "molded" into a spaceship - in astral form.

You need to realise that an atom is alive. It has a Logos with it.
It is also possible to mould astral atoms together to create something, just as you take atoms and create whatever you think you need.

So, in the astral realms, the living atoms that created a personality bundle, plus any extra atoms that might have been needed, where taken and placed around the astral form of the ship that had been made in thought form.

So, we don't know if you can follow this but these true aliens got volunteer personality bundles, made the form, in thought form, of a spaceship and, if you like, grew the spaceship, rather as a female grows a baby on Earth, around a life form created in the astral realms and projected into 3D reality.

The main difference was that all this was occurring in the astral realms.
There was nothing physical… yet!

We also wish to remind you, that as the volunteer personality bundle was and is alive, and all the atoms were and are alive, so the spaceship is alive.

If you can imagine a human being in astral form being alive, this is exactly the same but the "person" looks like a spaceship, rather than a human.

So, now we have a living entity that has taken the form of a flying craft.
It is in astral form but is a copy of the plans originally created on Earth a long time ago, by an advanced terrestrial civilization that no longer exist.

We should also mention that certain modifications were made to the original plans; (a) because in the astral realms, certain aspects created in a terrestrial craft would not be needed, and; (b) some of our friends have advanced knowledge and were able to suggest modifications that would improve the efficiency of the living craft, all in the astral realms.

So, we would like to repeat one more time the process of this, largely positive group, that decided to create spaceships to explore Earth.

A spacecraft made by this group is, in fact, a personality bundle not being used by a person, who volunteered to take the form of a craft first imagined by an advanced Earth race long ago that no longer exist.

The personality bundle was molded around the thought concept of a spacecraft, certain modifications were made and so it is now a living, thinking personality bundle that looks like, in the astral realms, a flying craft.

But, it is alive, has access to its Higher Self, Imagination and all the attributes that you have. The difference being that it's exterior and interior appearance is of a spacecraft.

It needs no one to fly it. It requires no motor, no fuel.
It is nourished in exactly the same manner as it would be had it remain just a personality bundle.
It is just a personality bundle pretending to be a spacecraft.

So, let us move onto the subject of this chapter which is how these living spacecraft travel.

First you must always bear in mind that they live in the astral realms, also called auras, and are made of vibration, the same vibration as the astral realm or aura that they lived in before transforming into a spacecraft.
Vibration is a subset of light and so these spacecraft vibrate to the frequency of that aura and are basically light.
You are also although, you may not realise it!

As we have said;
(a) The astral realms are all around us.
(b) If a person wishes to explore an astral realm, he creates a copy of himself, which he sends to the chosen astral realm, while his physical body stays in 3D, as it is called.

So, a spacecraft (from this group) does the same but in reverse.
It remains in the astral realms but creates a copy of itself, which it lowers in vibration so as to appear in our dimension.

However, in the astral realms, it is made of light and so when it appears in our dimension, it still has a certain connection to its astral double and would be seen by us in the sky as being, at least partly, as made of light.

People have seen such craft and have wondered why they appeared as if made of light, transparent or at least translucent.

It is quite simply that the personality bundle that is attempting to lower its frequency to our vibration, may not have completely mastered the technique and so does not appear entirely solid in our reality.

As regards travel, it does not travel. It is already in an aura that surrounds Earth and merely alters its frequency and it appears in our reality.

As we have said before, if the personality bundle pretending to be a spacecraft does not have complete mastery of changing its frequency, it will be seen to blink into our sky as a craft party made of light, then it will blink out again and disappear as it loses that connection to our frequency and blink in again as the personality bundle tries to retake control and so on.

We also say that, in the rare case of a personality bundle having total control or being able to enter our vibration, it would be seen as a solid craft, although there would be no one flying it and could not crash nor be shot down.
If it were to be attacked, it would immediately return to its first form in the astral realm and would disappear in an instant from our skies.

Once in our (your) reality - we are looking at things from your point of view - it would wish to explore the world.
The easiest way that this craft could do it is to return to the astral realm, pick another spot on Earth and appear at that point.

You may have heard of people doing astral projection and although they are only in the etheric realm, they instantly move to a chosen destination.
Equally, people that have visited the heavenly spheres, talk about being able to move about just by thought, desire to go to a new location.

A true spaceship can do this - travel by thought, desire to visit a new location.

Also, they can use the signalling posts that the builder race have placed both on planet Earth and also around the galaxy.
Or, use the vibrational points that are available throughout the galaxy, but we will explain these two ways of travelling more fully when we describe the Grey ships.

So, with regard to these true spaceships, made of light, with regard to how they travel, there is not much to say because, quite simply, they travel by thought.

As these ships are every bit as alive as you are, indeed one of them might be part of you, a personality bundle not being used by you and, as it is in constant telepathic communication with all people in the astral realms - all is one - everything that this living spaceship experiences is transmitted to the living library - the Akashic Record - and is available to all who are interested in following the ship and experience what it experiences.

We repeat, it is not often that a personality bundle that has taken the form of a spaceship is seen by people on Earth.

During the daytime, as they are made from light, they would be invisible, just blending into the sunlight, but at night-time they are occasionally seen as glowing shapes in the night sky, looking more or less like a standard UFO, depending on the attitude that the personality bundle adopts.

If there is one, or more than one, person who is/are projecting thoughts of interacting with this personality bundle (although, of course, those watching this object in the night sky would have no idea of what they are looking at, just thinking that it is a beautiful sparkling spaceship), the personality bundle might decide to change form and appear as a sort of human - which it is of course.

However, it is not easy, without a lot of training, to change dimensions, change form and appear as a solid object in our world.
So, they tend to appear as a glowing shape, vaguely human looking, and people who have photographed them are surprised and amazed that, if they send out a request to see the ship as a being, a few minutes later there is this very impressive, scintillating, glowing entity, vaguely human looking that appears in answer to their request.

Quite what these amazed people, clicking away with their cameras, would think if they knew that what they are endeavoring to capture in their cameras is actually an unused personality aspect of someone, is hard to imagine.

Many think that what they are looking at is a very advanced group of people from some distant star system and others think that they are looking at angelic beings.

Neither version is correct.

What they are observing, is an unused personality aspect contained in one of the dimensions, that has volunteered to take the form of a spaceship and enter our 3D world, to observe what we do down here and send the information back to the astral world in order to satisfy the curiosity of other personality bundles, wondering about interested in us - rather like we are interested in the astral realms.

So, they don't really travel, usually.
They use the power of thought, desire in a way, to move from place to place.

The spaceships have no engines because, as they are living aspects of creation, the power of God animates the created spaceship form, just as the power of God animates you.
You have no engine keeping you going. The heart pumps, it is true, to distribute oxygen and other elements around your body, but, have you ever wondered what power keeps the heart working?
That is the invisible power source that we call the power of God.

So, having explained at some length what a true space ship is and explained at a much lesser extent how it travels, as there is not much to say about these light ships, let us now turn to the other, Grey spaceships (UFO) and see if we can unravel the mystery surrounding them and their mode of transport.

We have already explained much, indeed most, of what needs to be said about these "Grey" ships, so much of what we would say would be a repeat but we will just remind you of the main points.

A long time ago, a demonic force decided to try to enter the physical world, in which you live, and to try to create a hybrid person with a human body and a demonic mind. Although demons have largely been misunderstood, it is known that they live in the lower fourth dimension and can only very rarely interact with humans at all and humans having an Earthly incarnation even less.

It has become increasingly popular for people, during their incarnation, to experience a problem and immediately jump to the conclusion that they are possessed by a demon of some sort.
If it was as easy as that, virtually all the demons would be overshadowing people all the time.

In fact, it is virtually impossible for a demon to overshadow a human, which is why they wanted to create hybrids in order to have a presence here on Earth.
As we have said, they will never be allowed to accomplish this feat.

Even a black magician has to train for many long years in order to be able to make contact with the least of the demons.

However, we wish to remind you also that, long years ago, planet Earth and its population was in the grip of dark forces, as the great pendulum swing of life waves slowly back and forth from dark to light, evil to holy.

At the time we are considering, there was a civilization around that had developed space travel. This race no longer exists but was the very same race that were traced by the personality bundles we mentioned earlier, discovered in the Akashic Records and that the plans were copied by these personality bundles.

But, at that long distant time, as Earth was deep within the folds of the negative period, it was fairly easy for the demonic forces to influence the scientists of that time to create solid, physical spaceships, that we will term UFO, to delineate them from those created by the personality bundles.

So, a long time ago, these scientists created, using the materials and technology that were available then and still are in the secret bases that were created long ago, physical spaceships, that we will refer to as UFO as opposed to spacecraft.

Thus, when seen in the skies or on the ground, they are seen as physical objects, as opposed to light craft and can crash or be shot down. They are entirely physical, although the technology used, based on the technology available long years ago, is far in advance than anything created by today's scientists.

We explained all this in a previous chapter.

But let us examine how they navigate either around Earth or throughout space.

We have already explained most of this but will do so again so as to complete this chapter.

The whole of our galaxy is composed of vibrations. Actually, there are both visible (under an electron microscope) and invisible atoms, known as dark matter.
They all vibrate to a certain frequency, which has nothing to do with the atoms waiting to be called into service, in order to assist in the creation of something.
These atoms have a different function but the important point - in this discussion - is that they all have a unique frequency so, if one knows the frequency of a particular atom at a particular point in the galaxy, it is possible to link with that vibration, in which case the person, UFO or whatever, ceases to be where it was and jumps to that new spot, the place where a particular atom is.

We have explained this in various essays and at least one video and we refer you to that information if you do not understand.
Thus, a UFO can jump instantly to any point both in the galaxy or on Earth, if it should require so to do.

Some people have noticed UFO hopping across the sky rather as a frog hops and what the UFO is doing is choosing a point either just a bit in advance of its present position - or at a vast distance - bombards the craft with a new frequency and the craft instantly hops to that new position.

The force deciding is, of course, the demonic entity that remains in the lower fourth dimension and projects its thoughts, either to the controls of the craft, rather like using radio control or by using PLFs that may be on board the UFO.

Other than that, a different but similar system is to use a sort of satellite navigation system that uses pyramids or similar masses of material - rocks - placed on planets throughout the galaxy.
As these masses of rock would vibrate to a certain unique frequency, the UFO can locate a frequency and jump to that spot.
It is very similar to the previous system we mentioned above but is also not unlike the satellite navigation system used on Earth at the moment.

So, we wish you to realise that a UFO can just cruise around if the powers controlling it wish but it can also and, usually, be guided from spot to spot using frequencies as we have just mentioned.

The last mentioned method is more frequently used, because the demonic aliens in the lower fourth like to know exactly where their UFO are at any moment and do not wish to chance losing contact with one of them, which could happen if they just let it cruise around.

We will not attempt to describe the power system(s), because there is more than one and all of them would be outside of any knowledge that you might have of anti-gravity flight, thus it would be pointless in us trying to describe them to you.

So, in this chapter we have attempted to explain both types of craft and their different methods of navigation.

CHAPTER 17

IN CLOSING

We will bring this book to a close.
We have done our best to dispel the myths surrounding the long-held beliefs that aliens and their various craft come from diverse planets and all sorts of old wives' tales, that have grown up around this concept, i.e.; meeting with all sorts of aliens; Pleiadians, Sirians and many other entities from any other star galaxy.

As time goes on, and as Internet expands, so people invent wilder and wilder stories concerning aliens, all based on the premise that they are physical beings, living on physical planets.

One wonders why people invent such tales but if one considers that to become famous, to sell books and to negotiate the lecture circuit, one needs a story of some kind to sell and so, people group together and agree to sell similar stories that the public seem only too willing to accept, and thus a small but growing group of people are continuing and pushing the limits to ever more fantastic degrees, in an attempt to be at the forefront of sensationalist news.

The problem is, of course, that eventually someone will go beyond the limits of the believable and the bubble will burst and the whole story will crash to the ground, because most of what is stated today is fiction presented as fact.

Of course, we take a different point of view and do our utmost to present truth, no matter what subject we are discussing.
We have no intention of seeking fame or fortune.
We are not interested in sensationalism.
We are interested in presenting to you, truth.

Now, we will be the first to admit, that what we have stated concerning aliens and their various craft reads like pure science fiction and not many of you will be able to accept it as fact.

But, as we mentioned elsewhere in this book, it is easier to accept untruth - that aliens come from some far distant galaxies - then the truth that we have exposed to you in this book.

We give this book to you, the general public, in the hopes that it will eventually bring knowledge concerning aliens to you, but we also do this to help a certain group of a secret service, who have discovered that aliens are interdimensional beings and are struggling to comprehend the true nature of aliens.

We know that they follow our teachings, as far as they relate to their mission, and as this book directly relates to the subject they are researching, we hope that this will help them in their investigations.

The problem is that, as all that we have written in this book is based on life forms in the astral realms, it is only by going into the astral realms that one can uncover the truth. There is virtually nothing physical to see, except for a few physical Grey craft and a few Grey PLF.

True aliens are entirely non-physical and so it is only those people who have psychic gifts developed that could enter the non-physical realms.

We are willing to help all people grow in wisdom and so we do what we can to assist all people to understand the truth about life, some of which is physical and much of which is astral.

In fact, of course, it is all astral, but one aspect seems physical.

So, we hope that you have read this book, even if you cannot accept all of it, you will be able to accept parts of it.
That which you cannot accept must remain outside of your belief.

However, it happens to be the truth and so, with time, people will come to accept what we have told you as true and mankind will advance in knowledge one more step.

So, we asked the blessing of Almighty God on your journey.

ADDENDUM

Q&A

Q1:
Bottom of page 136 mentions a "secret service". Are we (the readers) allowed to know more about this group?
The book was dedicated to them to because they were studying aliens and are currently confused.

A1:
This group are called "secret" because they are working in secret to try to discover just what aliens are.
It is not for us to break their secrecy.
But we will say that their intentions are purely from a research point of view and they do not intend any harm to anyone.
They are merely trying to resolve the mystery of who aliens are and we are happy to give them some pointers.

****

Q2:
In this book "Aliens" you said that it is pre-decided what atoms or elements are attracted to us and the rest of it is rejected by the body.
Now, if that is the case, then why are people diagnosed with some health problems, because of pollution?

A2:
The air that you breathe is meant to be pure and to contribute to a healthy body.
Naturally, the Archons, some hundreds of years ago realise that if they could pollute the air it would cause ill health and death.
If we take a piece of wood and burn it, atoms are released. This is a natural process.
The atoms in a piece of wood, if it is not burnt, remain with the wood until it gradually rots and the atoms are gently released in a harmless fashion.
However, if a piece of wood is burnt, the atoms are projected into the atmosphere in a violent manner, seen as smoke which is not designed to be ingested by man.
Thus, if man breathes this smoke, the atoms which should not be in the air and thus not ingested by man are breathed in and thus cause illness.
The atoms of a piece of wood have no connection to man - you do not eat wood - and so it just happens that if you breathe in atoms of wood, although you reject them, they can cause upset in the human body.
The same applies to coal, oil-based products, etc.
Any product that man is not designed to eat, drink or breathe, if ingested in anyway, will cause illness.

****

Q3:
Are some Greys good?

A3:
There is no such thing as a good Grey alien.
The little PLFs do not have personalities as they are just robots and the demonic forces that control them are, by nature, negative.
If any action by a demon produces positivity, it is by accident and not by design.

****

Q4:
If they don't have physical bodies, why do we call Reptilians, Reptilians?

A4:
Now, Reptilians, just like humans, are non-physical in nature.
Please do not forget that, just because there appears to be a few billion humans incarnate on planet Earth, that all humans are physical.
The vast majority of us remain in astral form.
In the case of Reptilians, they are non-physical, just as we are and their home is in the etheric realms.
So, if we recapitulate, our home is the higher 4th dimension.
The home of demons is the lower 4th dimension and the home of Reptilians is the etheric realms.
From there they can overshadow chosen people and influence them to carry out their agenda.
But, it is possible for them to so overshadow some evil people, that the person appears to take on the form of a Reptilian.
The body shape of Reptilians dates back a long time and will be fully explained one day but it is not for the moment.
We wish to finish the tasks we have been sent before branching off to other topics.

****

Q5:
Since there are Reptilians in Mars's atmosphere, do Reptilians count as aliens?

A5:
We could call Reptilians aliens but they are not really as they started out on Earth, as we will explain one day.
To be an alien implies being non-terrestrial. There are a large number of creatures unknown to man that live in the etheric realm surrounding Earth and Reptilians are one of them.
So, they are not considered by us to be aliens.

****

Q6:
What is the role of these true aliens in shaping human history.

A6:
If these good aliens that visit us have any influence at all, it is always to promote peace.
No positive group of beings would wish for the planet Earth to be annihilated by nuclear war, nor to have its population wiped out.
All life is intertwined and if human, animal and plant life was eliminated, planet Earth herself would cease to be. All is one.
Life is very important, so it is vital that all life should continue.
But, other than warning the military not to use nuclear weapons, good aliens, usually, just observe us.

****

Q7:
An alien race gave the Ten Commandments to Moses, seen by remote viewers. True or false?

A7:
This is a difficult question to answer as, although Moses was a real person, much of what is written about him is allegorical. So, the story of the Ten Commandments and the tablets of stone is allegorical - it never really happened.
We need to understand that the Akashic Record stores everything; every word, thought, writing, speech, etc.
So, when religious people invented the rules by which their religion should abide, they invented the story of Moses and that these rules for living were dictated by God and written in blocks of stone to give credence to their rules.
In fact, it was the creators of certain religions who made up the rules you know as the Ten Commandments.
Overtime, conventional wisdom has accepted that these tablets of stone existed and were given by an external force and so files have been created in the Akashic Record that supports that story.
The files were, and are, created by many people who accept without question the concept of the tablets being created by a higher source.
The remote viewers who looked at this event linked with collective wisdom and thus reported seeing the tablets produced by an external force. With their imaginations they visualized ET's creating the stones and that is what they reported.
But they were mistaken.
The Ten Commandments were written, created, by man.

****

Q8:

Did bad aliens influence the bad Egyptians?

A8:

You can be sure that behind any evil act is psychotic people influenced by evil forces. We will not say that the Grey aliens played any part in the slavery of captured people but the Archons, Reptilians and demonic beings serve the same negative agenda, so the demons will not be far away when slavery was going on.

****

Q9:

Can good aliens work for Archangels?

A9:

The answer is both yes and no.
In principle, as all life is one and all life is connected, there is nothing stopping any positive force working with positive Archangels, just as negative entities can be influenced by negative Archangels.
In practice, the difference in levels of spirituality, wisdom, etc., prevents any direct contact in either direction.

****

Q10:

When did humans separate into males and females? Who did it, good aliens during the Lemurian root race?

A10:

First, we would like to say that one needs to be careful when putting history into boxes and talking about root races appearing at certain times in history.
The history of human life on Earth doesn't progress quite like that, as we have tried to explain.
Also, male and female species; human, animal and plant, were constructed long ago by the Archangels, who seeded planet Earth with life. It was obvious that, for life to procreate, a mixture of different DNA was required and thus male/female was thought of. But it was thought of long, long ago and has nothing to do with so-called root races.

****

Printed in Great Britain
by Amazon

57966233R00079